THE RETIREMENT REFORMATION

Finding Freedom with Faith....
A Better Way to Experience the Final
(and Best) Decades of Your Life

BRUCE BRUINSMA

WESTBOW
PRESS®
A DIVISION OF THOMAS NELSON
& ZONDERVAN

WestBow Press books may be ordered through booksellers or by contacting:

WestBow Press
A Division of Thomas Nelson & Zondervan
1663 Liberty Drive
Bloomington, IN 47403
www.westbowpress.com
1 (866) 928-1240

ISBN: 978-1-9736-6173-3 (sc)
ISBN: 978-1-9736-6172-6 (hc)
ISBN: 978-1-9736-6174-0 (e)

Library of Congress Control Number: 2019907018

Print information available on the last page.

WestBow Press rev. date: 6/7/2019

Entering the Retirement Reformation

Mitch Anthony:

"There are many out there who instruct us how to have the means to retire but few who show us how have meaning in retirement. Bruce has written a meaning-full book on the topic.

None of us was born with a 'use-by' date stamped on us—we must fully live at every stage of life."

Mitch Anthony
Author, *The New Retirementality*
5th edition coming in 2020
Member of Retirement Reformation Roundtable

Hans Finzel:

"The Retirement Reformation is upon us. We are no longer living to just 65, retiring and dying. No, there is a huge new life beyond our main act careers. Life expectancy for most of us today is into the middle 80's. Thanks Bruce Bruinsma for pulling together a lot of subject matter experts relating to retiring with purpose in these last decades of our lives. These are the collected thoughts and essays of many men and women who have given a lot of thought and brainpower to a new way to look at our retirement years. I highly commend this book to you and your network!"

Dr. Hans Finzel,
Author and leadership mentor, *Launch Your Encore*
Member of Retirement Reformation Roundtable

Bill Tamulonis:

"Why are Baby Boomers the loneliest generation? Why are the oldest among us the least satisfied with life? *The Retirement Reformation* builds a convincing case, based on biblical and social-science data, that the reasons have much to do with buying into "the void of nothingness" that defines retirement for many. Thankfully, Bruce Bruinsma also offers an alternative perspective of retirement and a roadmap for how we can live the final season of life with purpose, meaning, and to the glory of God."

Bill Tamulonis
Managing Director
Acts Center for Applied Research
Member of Retirement Reformation Roundtable

Eric Thurman:

"Important movements take time to build, but the public suddenly becomes aware of them at some point. The movement appears to burst on the scene, though it was years in the making. A reformation about retirement is such a movement. Thought leaders have been working independently on the subject for years. Now, we are uniting to wave a banner together for a few key principles. It is time for a Great Awakening about retirement because tens of millions of people are entering into mature adulthood dangerously unaware of its challenges or opportunities. We feel we are on the cusp of an awakening. This book and its stories are important expressions of key issues about retirement that, we agree, need to be front and center in everyone's attention."

Eric Thurman
Author, *THRIVE in RETIREMENT*
Member of Retirement Reformation Roundtable

Bruce Peppin:

"There is a move of God sweeping across thought leaders today to redefine our understanding of retirement. Millions of baby boomers who are entering their later years will soon gain a new vision and be redeployed to serving Christ's call of 'Follow Me!' *The Retirement Reformation* by Bruce Bruinsma is at the forefront of this new movement. Read it and be inspired for your future!"

Bruce Peppin
Author, *The Best Is Yet to Be!* F
Founder of FinishingLifeWell.com.
Member of Retirement Reformation Roundtable

Richard and Leona Bergstrom:

"Would you like to know a seasoned and knowledgeable financial advisor who recognizes a successful retirement plan consists of far more than acquiring wealth? Meet Bruce Bruinsma, author of the book, *The Retirement Reformation*—and founder of the movement by the same name. Written from the depths of his heart and experience, you will walk with Bruce through his journey to discover meaning and purpose in a new season of life. You'll feel the passion of his personal calling and convictions, and you'll be challenged to reframe your own perceptions of retirement. Apply the Biblically based principles and practical suggestions and you will experience what it means to reform retirement!"

Richard and Leona Bergstrom
Co-Authors, *Third Calling: What are you doing the rest of your life?*
Member of Retirement Reformation Roundtable

Brian Kluth:

"Bruce Bruinsma has sounded the trumpet for Christians everywhere to rethink, refocus and reprioritize their retirement years. Rather than being years of living only for pleasure or doing nothing, this book will help you live your legacy years, so they are filled with meaning and purpose as God used you to make the lives of others #BetterForever."

Brian Kluth
Generosity Speaker and Author, *Christian Legacy Organizer*
Member of Retirement Reformation Roundtable

Amy Hanson:

"Full of inspiration, real life examples, and a strong Biblical focus, this book will challenge and inspire you to steward your retirement years for the glory of God!"

Amy Hanson, Ph.D.
Author, *Baby Boomers and Beyond*
Member of Retirement Reformation Roundtable

Wes Wick:

"*The Retirement Reformation* helps us rethink retirement and invigorates us to not squander the last third of our lives. We can't get swindled by the false narrative and low expectations of our entitlement culture! This book is written by a man who practices what he preaches. Allow Bruce's sage voice of wisdom and experience to challenge you to experience God's best in retirement. Fresh, timely, well-beyond-financial advice for those in retirement or making plans."

Wes Wick
Co-Founder/Director, YES! Young Enough to Serve
yestoserve.org
Member of Retirement Reformation Roundtable

Jon Hirst

"The Retirement Reformation takes an expansive look at how Christians should live in retirement. But it doesn't stay at 30,000 feet. Instead Bruce Bruinsma dives into key areas of life that are deeply practical and provides helpful insight to navigate this significant portion of 21st Century life."

Jon Hirst
Executive Director
The Generous Mind, Releasing Ideas to the World
Key contributor to The Retirement Reformation Movement

INTRODUCTION TO THE
RETIREMENT REFORMATION

Paul Tornier wrote, *Success in retirement depends in great measure on the way we lived beforehand.*

Howard Hendrix wrote: *Change is always a challenge to one's faith, and there is no faith without risk.* He also wrote, *Retirement … is the chance to do everything that leads to nothing.*

Challenge, change, risk, success, and the void of nothingness. All issues surrounding todays struggle with what the world calls Retirement. Adopting a new normal without consulting God's plan for our lives leads to the current void so many find in those last decades of life. The current American dream of Retirement is synonymous with freedom. Unfortunately, too often it is framed within a context of *freedom from*, with little thought about what this freedom will lead to … *freedom to* is only an afterthought.

Paul Tournier saw the issue starting to take shape in the 70's highlighted in his book, "Learn to Grow old." Then Harold Hendricks addressed it with great insight in his W. H. Griffith Thomas lectures at Dallas Theological Seminary. Bob Buford's book published in 1995, Half-Time, raised the issues brought about by key life transitions. Insights into the challenges of going from success to significance helped frame our discussions in the 90's. Issues of grandparenting and intergenerational relationships came to the front in the early 2000's. Now there are emerging thought leaders delving into all aspects of the new reality brought on by observable longevity.

In 2009, John Piper*, pastor and prolific author, began to address the issues of Retirement in our culture. He connected God's heart and plan to the emerging reality of longevity and cultural emptiness. Here is an excerpt from his booklet Rethinking Retirement, "Finishing life for the glory of Christ."

Getting old to the glory of God means resolutely resisting the typical American dream of retirement. It means being so satisfied with all that God promises to be for us in Christ that we are set free from the cravings that create so much emptiness and uselessness in retirement. Instead, knowing that we have an infinitely satisfying and everlasting inheritance in God just over the horizon of life makes us zealous in our few remaining years here to spend ourselves in the sacrifices of love, not the accumulation of comforts.

In John 21:19, Jesus told Peter "by what kind of death he was to glorify God." There are different ways of dying. And there are different ways of living just before we die. But for the Christian all of them—the final living, and the dying—are supposed to make God look glorious. All of them are supposed to show that Christ—not this world—is our supreme Treasure.

So, growing old to the glory of God means using whatever strength and eyesight and hearing and mobility and resources we have left to treasure Christ and in that joy to serve people—that is seek to bring them with us into the everlasting enjoyment of Christ. Serving people, and not ourselves, as the overflow of treasuring Christ makes Christ look great.

One of the great obstacles to getting old to the glory of God is the fear that we will not persevere in treasuring Christ and loving people—we just won't make it. We won't be able to say with Paul in 2 Timothy 4:7-8, "I have fought the good fight, I have finished the race, I have kept the faith. Henceforth there is laid up for me the crown of righteousness, which the Lord, the righteous judge, will award to me on that Day, and not only to me but also to all who have loved his appearing." The reward of final righteousness will come to those who have loved his appearing, that is, who treasure him supremely and want him to be here. So, this treasuring of Christ must be included in and part of the fought-fight and the finished-race and the kept-faith. Faith includes treasuring Christ and his appearing. You don't have faith if you don't want Jesus.

So, one great obstacle to getting old to the glory of God is the fear that we can't maintain this treasuring of Christ. And so we can't bear the fruit of love that flows from faith (Galatians 5:6; 1 Timothy 1:5). We're not going to make it.

So, what is the right way to overcome the fear of not persevering in old age? The key is to keep finding in Christ our highest Treasure. This is not mainly the fight to *do* but the fight to *delight*. We keep on looking away from ourselves to Christ for his blood-bought fellowship and his help. Which means we keep on believing. We keep on fighting the fight of faith by looking at Christ and valuing Christ and receiving Christ every day.

Spurgeon says that God kisses away the fear of aging with his promises. Philippians 1:6: "I am sure of this, that he who began a good work in you will bring it to completion at the day of Jesus Christ." 1 Corinthians 1:8-9: "[He] will sustain you to the end, guiltless in the day of our Lord Jesus Christ. God is faithful, by whom you were called into the fellowship of his Son, Jesus Christ our Lord." Jude 1:24: "[He] is able to keep you from stumbling and to present you blameless before the presence of his glory with great joy." Romans 8:30: "Those whom he predestined he also called, and those whom he called he also justified, and those whom he justified he also glorified." No one is lost between justification and glorification. All who are justified are glorified. The point of telling us that is to kiss away all fear. If God is for us, no one can successfully be against us (Romans 8:31).

Therefore, perseverance is necessary for final salvation, and perseverance is certain for all those who are in Christ. The works we do on the path of love do not win God's favor. They result from God's favor. Christ won God's favor. And we receive him by faith alone. And love is the overflow and demonstration of this faith.

This is the key to growing old to the glory of God. If we are going to make God look glorious in the last years of our lives, we must be satisfied in him. He must be our Treasure. And the life that we live must flow from this all-satisfying Christ. And the life that flows from the soul that lives on Jesus is a life of love and service. This is what will make Christ look great. When our hearts find their rest in Christ, we stop using other people to meet our needs, and instead we make ourselves servants to meet their needs. This is so contrary to the unregenerate human heart that it stands out as something beautiful to be followed or something convicting to be crucified.

It works both ways. Polycarp, the bishop of Smyrna illustrates both and what it may mean for us to grow old to the glory of God.

Polycarp was the Bishop of Smyrna in Asian Minor. He lived from about AD 70 to 155. He is famous for his martyrdom which is recounted in *The Martyrdom of Polycarp* and found in Henry Bettenson's *Documents of the Christian Church* (Oxford, 1967, pp. 9-12). Tensions had risen between the Christians and those who venerated Caesar. The Christians were called atheists because they refused to worship any of the Roman gods and had no images or shrines of their own. At one point, a mob cried out, "Away with the atheists; let search be made of Polycarp."

At a cottage outside the city, he remained in prayer and did not flee. He had a vision of a burning pillow and said to his companion, "I must needs be burned alive." The authorities sought him, and he was betrayed to them by one of his servants under torture. He came down from an upper room and talked with his accusers. "All that were present marveled at his age and constancy, and that there was so much ado about the arrest of such an old man" (p. 9). He asked for permission to pray before being taken away. They allowed it and "being so filled with the grace of God that for two hours he could not hold his peace" (p. 10).

In the town, the sheriff met him and took him into his carriage and tried to persuade him to deny Christ, "Now what harm is there in saying 'Lord Caesar,' and in offering incense … and thus saving thyself?" He answered, "I do not intend to do what you advise." Angered, they hastened him to the stadium where there was a great tumult.

The proconsul tried again to persuade him to save himself, "Have respect to thine age … Swear by the genius of Caesar … Repent … Say, 'Away with the atheists! [that is, Christians]." Polycarp turned to the "mob of lawless heathen in the stadium, and he waved his hand at them, and looking up to heaven he groaned and said, 'Away with the atheists.'" Again, the proconsul said, "Swear, and I will release thee; curse the Christ." To this Polycarp gave his most famous response, "Eighty and six years have I served him, and he hath done me no wrong; how then can I blaspheme my king who saved me?"

The proconsul said again, "Swear by the genius of Caesar." And Polycarp answered, "If thou dost vainly imagine that I would swear by the genius of Caesar, as thou sayest, pretending not to know what I am, hear plainly that I am a Christian." The proconsul replied, "I have wild beasts; if thou repent not, I will throw thee to them." To which Polycarp replied, "Send for them. For repentance from better to worse is not a change permitted to us; but to change from cruelty to righteousness is a noble thing" (p. 11).

The proconsul said, "If thou doest despise the wild beasts I will make thee to be consumed by fire, if thou repent not." Polycarp answered, "Thou threatenest the fire that burns for an hour and in a little while is quenched; for thou knowest not of the fire of the judgment to come, and the fire of the eternal punishment, reserved for the ungodly. But why delayest thou? Bring what thou wilt."

The proconsul sent word that it should be proclaimed aloud to the crowd three times, "Polycarp hath confessed himself to be a Christian." After the crowd found out that there were no beasts available for the task, they cried out for him to be burned alive. The wood was gathered, and as they were about to nail his hands to the timber he said, "Let me be as I am. He that granted me to endure the fire will grant me also to remain at the pyre unmoved, without being secured with nails." The fire did not consume him, but an executioner drove a dagger into his body. "And all the multitude marveled at the great difference between the unbelievers and the elect." (p. 12).

When we are so satisfied in Christ that we are enabled to willingly die for him, we are freed to love the lost as never before, and Christ is shown to be a great Treasure.

When I got prostate cancer and had surgery last year at age 60, I recalled the experience of Charles Simeon and prayed that his outcome would be true for me.

Simeon was the pastor of Trinity Church, Cambridge, two hundred years ago. He learned a very painful lesson about God's attitude toward his "retirement." In 1807, after 25 years of ministry at Trinity Church, his health broke when he was 47. He became very weak and had to take an extended leave from his labor. Handley Moule recounts the fascinating story of what God was doing in Simeon's life.

The broken condition lasted with variations for thirteen years, till he was just sixty, and then it passed away quite suddenly and without any evident physical cause. He was on his last visit to Scotland ... in 1819, and found himself, to his great surprise, just as he crossed the border, "almost as perceptibly renewed in strength as the woman was after she had touched the hem of our Lord's garment."

He says that he had been promising himself, before he began to break down, a very active life up to sixty, and then a Sabbath evening [retirement!]; and that now he seemed to hear his Master saying: "I laid you aside, because you entertained with satisfaction the thought of resting from your labor; but now you have arrived at the very period when you had promised yourself that satisfaction, and have determined instead to spend your strength for me to the latest hour of your life, I have doubled, trebled, quadrupled your strength, that you may execute your desire on a more extended plan."4

How many Christians set their sights on a "Sabbath evening" of life—resting, playing, traveling, etc.—the world's substitute for heaven since the world does not believe that there will be a heaven beyond the grave. The mindset or our peers is that we must reward ourselves now in this life for the long years of our labor. Eternal rest and joy after death is an irrelevant consideration. When you don't believe in heaven to come and you are not content in the glory of Christ now, you will seek the kind of retirement that the world seeks. But what a strange reward for a Christian to set his sights on! Twenty years of leisure (!) while living in the midst of the Last Days of infinite consequence for millions of people who need Christ. What a tragic way to finish the last mile before entering the presence of the king who finished his last mile so differently!

When I heard J. Oswald Sanders at the Trinity Evangelical Divinity School chapel speaking at the age of 89 say that he had written a book a year for Christ since he was 70, everything in me said, "O God, don't let me waste my final years! Don't let me buy the American dream of retirement—month after month of leisure and play and hobbies and putering around in the garage and rearranging the furniture and golfing and fishing and sitting and watching television. Lord, please have mercy on me. Spare me this curse."

That is my prayer for you as well. I close with a passion and a promise. The passion is Psalm 71:18—a passion to make the greatness of God known to the generations we are leaving behind: "Even to old age and gray hairs, O God, do not forsake me, until I proclaim your might to another generation, your power to all those to come." O that God would give us a passion in our final years to spend ourselves to make him look as great as he really is—to get old to the glory of God.

The promise: Isaiah 46:3-4, "[You] have been borne by me from before your birth, carried from the womb; even to your old age I am he, and to gray hairs I will carry you. I have made, and I will bear; I will carry and will save." Don't be afraid, Christian. You will persevere. You will make it home. Sooner than you think. Live dangerously for the one who loved you and died for you at age 33. Don't throw your life away on the American dream of retirement. You are as secure as Christ is righteous, and God is just. Don't settle for anything less than the joyful sorrows of magnifying Christ in the sacrifices of love. And then in the Last Day, you will stand and hear, "Well done good and faithful servant. Enter into the joy of your master."

*John Piper is founder and teacher of DesiringGod.org and chancellor of Bethlehem College & Seminary. For more than thirty years, he served as pastor of Bethlehem Baptist Church, Minneapolis. He is author of more than fifty books, and his sermons, articles, books, and more are available free of charge at desiringGod.org.

The Retirement Reformation is a movement, and this book by the same name leads the way to the next generation of understanding retirement from God's perspective today. Finding Freedom with Faith and learning how to experience what may be your greatest decades is the opportunity the book presents.

It also challenges all Faith based ministries, churches and para-church organizations to respond to the new realities of aging, the opportunities presented by the Retirement Reformation and to make room for thousands of Christians awakening to a new call on their life.

The Retirement Manifesto compiled by 15 Retirement Reformation Roundtable members, presents the issues and the basic principles of the movement succinctly and with clarity. It will challenge you with new perspectives about the last decades of our lives.

Paul Tournier, Howard Hendricks, Bob Buford and John Piper saw new issues and new paths. Bruce Bruinsma and the other Retirement Reformation Roundtable members bring the next generation of insight, vision and possibilities that will impact our changing world.

The Retirement Reformation
Finding Freedom with Faith … A Better Way to Experience
the Final (and Best) Decades of Your Life

John 15:16
*"You did not choose me, but I chose you and called you so
that you might bear fruit – fruit that will last – and whatever
you ask in My Father's name, He will give it to you."*

Romans 12:2
*Do not conform to the pattern of this world but be transformed
by the renewing of your mind. Then you will be able to test and
approve what God's will is—His good, pleasing and perfect will.*

Ephesians 4:16
*From Him, the whole body, joined and held together
by every supporting ligament, grows and builds
itself up in love, as each part does its work.*

CONTENTS

PREFACE

THE RETIREMENT REFORMATION

This book is not about money. Money suggests buying and selling, while this book is about being and doing. I have spent 30 years building a company, Envoy Financial, most of that time in conjunction with our daughter, Bethany. The journey has been so much more than building a company, it has been a response to God's call to help Jesus followers prepare financially for their future ministry when the paycheck stops.

The phrase, Future Funded Ministry, and the meaning behind it, has been part of my messaging and a personal focus for 25 years. This phrase encompasses key retirement issues and reframes our thoughts about the financial side of retirement. Retirement is in the future, each Christian's role as a Jesus representative (changed lives) never stops, and these last 30 years must be funded. Future Funded Ministry addresses the financial piece of the retirement equation. There is so much more.

I tried to write the definitive book about retirement and explain the idea of Future Funded Ministry on multiple occasions. I discovered two things as a result, I like writing, and each time the book started to form, I could not finish it. On the writing side, I have completed two smaller books dealing with the subject matter, and now written close to 300 blogs on related topics. Both Finding Freedom and Moving Forward were partially satisfying. On the larger, more definitive or complete book, I just wasn't ready.

The reason I wasn't ready was because God wasn't finished forming me into the person, I needed to be to write the book. The person I needed to be in order to reflect His content about this subject rather than my own, limited, understanding. We often talk about God's timing. It's true, there is a time and place for His will to be reflected in our lives in unique and often unusual ways. Solomon's reflection in the Biblical book of Ecclesiastes is right, "There is a season …". Now is the season for the expanded message of the Retirement Reformation.

A few years ago, Judy and I stood in St. Paul's cathedral in Rome and marveled at Michelangelo's Pieta. It brought wonder to my eyes and tears too. It spoke of a mother's passion and God's love. A few days later when we traveled to Florence, we again stood in awe of Michelangelo's powerful statue of David. Researching more about how these astounding works of art came to be, I read the story of how God worked through the sculpture to create something beautiful, something new, something impactful, and something reflecting Him. Michelangelo, when asked about the creative process said, "Every block of stone has a statue inside it, and it is the task of the sculptor to discover it". He also said, "I saw the angel in the marble and carved until I set him free."

The marble contained God's plan existing from eons of time, it was just waiting for His timing and His instrument to release a message to the world. I think about the Retirement Reformation in a similar vein. He's known about this time in history, its uniqueness, its challenges and its opportunities. The opportunities for each of us, and the roles each of us are to play. Each of us have been identified, called, prepared and need to be ready to move into a new stage of Kingdom work. Each of us has a role to play, and The Retirement Reformation is one way, in our time, for those roles to be unearthed, envisioned, and acted upon.

Never since the extended lifetime of Methuselah, have we been given the luxury of so much life-time. Not only is life being extended in almost miraculous ways, but also our capacity to be productive is being extended. Judy and I are in our 57th year of marriage. She has survived and thrived through two child birth's, bouts with uterine and breast cancer, and open-heart surgery. Throughout all of recorded history, she would of, should have died, multiple times. Yet here she is, active, engaged and able to bring her editing skills and insights to this book. She reflects my grandmother's observation, "With all your faults I love you still". I'm thankful she still loves me, and it is certainly reciprocated. "Thank you dear, I love you."

God has certainly taken a long time to form and shape me into His vessel for delivering this part of the Retirement Reformation message. There are so many other voices that make up the chorus composing the Retirement Reformation. I'll return to them shortly. I won't take your through the twists and turns of my journey here, perhaps there will be another venue. However, some of the story is shared in the book, and the message of the Retirement Reformation is actually a reflection of my life's journey. It's not the details of the journey that are important, it is the message that emerges from the journey.

The 30-year journey to prompt faith-based organizations to set up retirement plans for their staff has had its share of frustrations. Frustrations both with the organization's response to the need, and then for the participants to engage with the process. The biggest frustration is getting Christians to acknowledge and engage with the need to prepare for the future financially. When we are prepared, we can be so much more effective is every area of life.

In 1959 Tom Lehrer wrote and performed a parody on the Boy Scout motto, Be Prepared. "Be prepared, as through life we march along, Be Prepared." While I can only smile at some of his lyrics, the motto applies to all of us, Be Prepared!

It took a lot of years for God to help me understand the unwillingness of so many to prepare financially for their future. While it seems obvious, the preparation by so many is insufficient to say the least. Here is the answer: The reason is that our "Why" isn't big enough. We all take action when our why is big enough, strong enough, and staring us in the face. When our tooth hurts enough, we go to the dentist. When enough people have lauded a particular movie or play, we go. When we've seen enough pictures of the Grand Canyon, we go and see for ourselves. When the hole in our soul gets big enough, we turn to God. This book explores the issues surrounding "Why". I think you will find yourself in the message. It is important to know your Why. It's the step that precedes the action plan.

It's our answer to "why" that drives us. Money is only a medium of exchange, it's not the Why. Our critical "why" explodes when we recognize that God does have a call on our lives, and it doesn't stop at 65, although so many of us act as if it does. Unfortunately, so many of us live our lives without ever recognizing or hearing the call, God's message for our lives. Our Why, what drives us, is truly God's call on our lives coupled with our subsequent response. Whether this insight is new to you, and your next step is connecting with God's plan for you, or you've known your why for a long time and just never acted on it? The Why leads to the passion to listen and act on God's call. For me my calling is to the Retirement Reformation. It is the culmination of His Call and all God has taught me though over 75 years of shaping. While this is my call, perhaps yours is connected to this mission too.

Just as a coastline is the result of ocean waves pounding on the shore, each of us is the result of the waves of life shaping who we are and therefore impacting what we will now do. When you add that shaping to the starting DNA, we are all becoming new creatures and each has a destiny, a role to play in growing God's kingdom. It is the pain of creation that leads to the beauty of new birth. It is true in nature; it is true in our lives. And, as Michelangelo reflected, "I am still learning."

The Retirement Reformation is a movement, not a book(s), a program or any one of the components that make up the supporting content, those sources are tributaries creating what will be a mighty river of reformation. My contribution is just one of those tributaries. Even this tributary is not mine alone but shaped by many others. The 30 years of Envoy relationships played a key role. Thank you, Bethany and so many others. Judy is a constant source of encouragement and insight. My Canadian partner in Laotian coffee and ministry, Vaden Williams, played a major role. The many who have joined in numerous church and ministry activities were key contributors. Jon Hirst has helped shape the thoughts about the Reformation, Steve Rabey has helped lighten the message and made it more fun and easier to connect the dots. The InChrist Communication team is critical to releasing the message to the world. Thanks to each and to all who have been part of my learning and growing process. A special thanks to The Unshackled Life group at our church for engaging with me on life's journey during these last years of Retirement Reformation formation. There will be many joining me, most I do not know, but God does. He has it all planned out; pray we follow his call.

And now for the implementation stage, the start of a new journey.

James 1:22
But prove yourselves doers of the word, and not merely hearers who delude themselves.

The Retirement Reformation Roundtable

Finally, a word about the Retirement Reformation Roundtable. This is a key group of thought leaders about Retirement Reformation related issues. Each and every one of them has been and is on their own journey. We have a couple of things in common. First, we are Jesus followers, and second, we've come face to face with the issues of longevity and how those issues are to be addressed in our times. Most have written extensively about related subjects. I'm so thankful to them for their willingness to share their journey and come together, joining hands as we walk into God's preferred future of the Retirement Reformation.

Sixteen of us came together in November of 2018 in Colorado Springs. Our mutual commitment was to share, learn from each other, and look into the future of the Retirement Reformation. This look included a commitment to stay connected, be supportive, and help lead the way to the Retirement Reformation.

Our next step was to create a statement reflecting the issues and direction the Reformation is to take: The Retirement Reformation Manifesto. Like the Declaration of Independence, it took a little while to draft, but as completed, it is a marvelous statement of the issues and principles that will guide the movement.

The Manifesto was created in two formats: One the complete statement, and the second a condensed version. Below is a copy of the complete statement, and the signatures of the Retirement Reformation Roundtable members. It is likely the Retirement Reformation Roundtable will add a few more members in the future. I am and always will be grateful to the initial band of believers who were willing to listen to the call and take next steps, together.

With the Manifesto in hand, we now ask you to consider joining the movement. Please read this book, and perhaps one or two others written by Retirement Reformation Roundtable members. Each book has an impactful message. Then go to RetirementReformation.org website and sign on as the newest member of the Retirement Reformation movement. There is a new and exciting journey ahead for each of us. Isn't it wonderful to know, that at the end of the journey, Jesus is waiting for us with open arms ready to affirm us as "Good and faithful servants." My prayer for each is "Let it be, Lord, let it be."

Bruce Bruinsma
Colorado Springs, CO

SECTION 1

"HOW IN THE WORLD DID WE GET HERE?"

CHAPTER 1

THE DINNER DATE

They had that deer-in-the-headlights look you can recognize when first-time visitors come to your church. We welcomed them warmly. I reached out to the man and Judy said hello to the woman. Both seemed to be in their fifties.

"So, what brings you to our church?" I asked.

"Well, we drove past this church the other day, so we actually know where it is and how to get here," said Dave, who explained he was a manager with one of the big home-improvement chains and had just been transferred to run a new store in Colorado Springs.

"We need to find a church home to go with our new home," said Terri, who had been involved in a Christian women's book club and a women's small group at the church they left behind in Topeka. Terri worked as a freelance technical writer and was scheduling interviews with local firms.

"We think you will like Colorado Springs," said Judy.

"This may just be the place where we finally get to settle down for a while," said Dave, who wanted his fifth new-store-transfer in twenty years to be his last.

"I sure hope so!" said Terri.

Judy and I were meeting our kids for lunch after church, so we couldn't hang around and talk after the service.

"Well," I asked, "how about if the four of us get together for coffee or dinner some time?"

"We would like that!" said Dave.

"That would be wonderful," said Terri. "We don't know a *soul* here." We scheduled dinner for the following Friday evening.

Breaking Bread

After the four of us ordered our meals, we started getting to know each other.

Dave and Terri had moved from city to city for Dave's work. Now they were two empty-nesters in their late fifties, and they were looking for a place to call home. They had raised three kids but remained in contact with only two of them. They shared a vague sense of sadness that they could have done better raising their children if they had given them more time and attention.

"I'm tired of being a vagabond," said Terri. "We're just hoping we could settle down here for more than five years,"

"And after what I've been through this week with our Human Resources office," said Dave, "I can't wait for retirement."

David didn't realize it, but when he said the word "retirement," alarm bells started going off in my head. I've spent decades working in the retirement industry. Envoy Financial, the company I founded with my daughter, Bethany, works with hundreds of churches and religious organizations to provide quality retirement plans to tens of thousands of their workers.

"What do you mean you can't wait?" I asked.

"Our company is changing employee retirement again," said Dave, "and the new material about all the choices and options is impossible to comprehend. How in the world did we get here with all these confusing retirement options? It's the kind of thing that makes me dream of hopping behind the wheel of an RV and heading off to the mountains."

"I'm not sure what Dave will do around the house all day," said Terri, "but I do get tired of how the company keeps yanking his chain all the time by changing his benefits."

"Let me ask you two a question," I said. "Do the two of you believe God has a plan for your life right now, in this stage of your life?"

"We believe it," said Terri, "but we're not sure what that is."

I'm on a mission to change the way people think about retirement.

The Confession

"I've got a confession to make," I said.

"I have spent my life working in the retirement industry. But don't worry. I'm not trying to sell you anything. My work is mainly with Christian ministries and churches, not individuals.

"But I'm also on a mission to change the way people think about retirement. I believe most people have it all wrong, and they're missing wonderful opportunities to serve God in their later years when they could be most effective serving His kingdom.

"I'm working on a book about all this and would love to sit down and pick your brains. Could the three of us do that sometime? I know Judy doesn't need to hear me talk about these ideas anymore. And like I said, I promise I'm not trying to sell you anything."

Dave and Terri looked at each other, then looked at me and said, "Well, that sounds like it could help us."

The three of us agreed to meet for lunch a couple weeks later.

Questions worth thinking about.

1. Have you had a conversation about retirement recently? With whom? About what?
2. Observing others in retirement, list three things you've noticed, wondered about, or raised issues for you:
   a. ?
   b. ?
   c. ?
3. Do you know someone who has done a great job of planning for retirement and is carrying it out? Make some notes about what you've observed.
4. Do you know someone who has not planned and is struggling as a result? Make some notes of what you've observed.

CHAPTER 2

PEOPLE DON'T PLAN FOR RETIREMENT

Dave and Terri slid into the booth at the restaurant, which was filling up with a lunch-time crowd. They had agreed to meet me so we could talk about retirement. After the three of us caught up and ordered lunch, I asked them a question.

"When we met for dinner a few weeks ago, the two of you said you had already done a fair amount of retirement planning," I said. "Can you spell out for me what kind of planning you have done?"

I had asked them to bring along any documents or retirement planning information they had, and Terri had spent a few hours organizing her big, thick retirement notebook. For the next five minutes, Dave and Terri led me through the extensive research they had done. Terri led me through her notebook, which included information on all their retirement accounts, including 401(k)s, IRAs, and Social Security accounts. The notebook also had a section containing a copy of their will, living trust, and other important documents.

"This is truly impressive!" I said. "I've talked to thousands of people about retirement, and few have been as organized or done as much research as you two have."

"Thanks," said Terri. "We're really proud of the work we've done to prepare."

"But I have one question for you. Do you have anything in that notebook that isn't about money?"

The two of them looked at each other, and then gave me a quizzical look.

"Not really," said Dave. "What do you mean?"

There's More to Retirement Than Money

I opened my laptop and Googled the words "retirement plan." In less than a second, I had more than a million results—the vast majority being links to major financial firms selling various investment products.

"I want you to look at something," I said, turning my laptop around so we could scroll through the results together. The Google search results were a catalog of companies selling retirement products and investments.

"Looking to Save For Retirement?" said one online ad. "Vanguard Can Help."

"Saving for Retirement Now Is the First Step. Let Voya Help You Get Started."

"Start preparing for your financial future with a retirement savings plan from Nationwide Financial."

"Plan for an Income That Lasts All of Your Retirement," said an ad from Prudential. "Start Here."

I could tell Dave and Terri were wondering where I was going.

"It's not surprising," I said. "After hearing millions of commercials and seeing millions of ads, all of us have been effectively trained. We have now largely accepted the idea that 'retirement planning' means 'financial planning.'

"What are you saying?" Terri asked me.

"Well, what I'm saying is that I talk to people every day who believe retirement planning means learning all about various investment options and products. These people can tell me all about traditional and Roth IRAs, defined-benefit plans, 401(k) plans, and other financial programs. But they've never really stopped to ask what it would take to use their retirement years to develop and use their God-given gifts and calling to achieve meaning and purpose."

I went to the Investopedia website and showed them the home page, which boldly declares its finances-only emphasis in its opening-sentence: "Retirement planning is the process of determining **retirement** *income* *goals* and the actions and decisions necessary to achieve those goals."

Financial planning is very important. But there's *much more* to retirement planning than financial planning.

"Wait a minute," Dave said. "Are you telling us that financial planning for retirement *isn't* important?"

"No, that's not it. Don't get me wrong. Financial planning is important. *Very* important. But there's more to retirement planning than financial planning. *Much* more. That's because men and women do not live by bread—or investment accounts—alone."

Dave and Terri looked at me and looked at their big retirement notebook. Clearly, financial planning was the only kind of retirement planning they had done. They're not alone. Financial planning is the only kind of retirement planning most of us do.

"I think it's great that the two of you have done all this planning to create your big, impressive retirement notebook," I said. "And I think it may be a good thing that financial firms bring people the message that planning is important. Perhaps some of those commercials and ads have encouraged you to do all the planning that you have done. So far, so good.

"But we're leaving out something important. I just wish people wouldn't limit their retirement planning to only financial issues. There's so much more to life than money, no matter what chapter of life we are living."

Creating Retirement

Dave listened to my argument about the need for both financial planning and life planning.

"So, how did we get here?" he asked, repeating his question from our dinner two weeks earlier. I took that as an invitation to present my brief lesson on the history of retirement.

It's no wonder that people find retirement planning challenging. It's not something we humans have been doing for very long. Throughout history, few people had any kind of reliable safety net for their later years. In fact, throughout history, few people even had later years.

One humorous story put it like this:

In the beginning, there was no retirement. There were no old people. In the Stone Age, everyone was fully employed until age 20, by which time nearly everyone was dead, usually of unnatural causes. Any early man who lived long enough to develop crow's-feet was either worshiped or eaten as a sign of respect ...

In those days, it was customary to carry on until you dropped, regardless of your age group -- no shuffleboard, no Airstream trailer. When a patriarch could no longer farm, herd cattle or pitch a tent, he opted for more specialized, less labor-intensive work, like prophesying and handing down commandments. Or he moved in with his kids.

People don't realize that up until four centuries ago, life expectancy remained low, and people considered themselves lucky if they made it to 40.

America's Social Security act was passed in 1935, largely as a response to the widespread losses people suffered in the Great Depression. Government economists set the retirement age at 65, even though Americans life expectancy at the time was only 58 years. But by 1960, Americans life expectancy had soared to almost 70 years.

Today, there are nearly 40 million retired Americans, and their longer life expectancies are part of what is driving the need for "retirement planning."

In 1960, a person retiring at 65 could expect only a few years of retirement. Today, similar retirees could be looking at 20 or 30 years of retirement. That's a much longer time, and it requires more resources, which is why financial firms emphasize financial planning.

But financial planning isn't the only kind of retirement planning people need to think about. Money is important, but it is only a means to an end: a financially stress-free retirement. Money is not the end in itself. The sooner we realize that, the sooner we can all begin doing the hard work of moving beyond means and thinking about ends. We can move beyond discussing investing in 401k's, 403(b) 's, or IRA's and start thinking about how we want to invest the last third of our lives.

"No Longer Productive"

Dave and Terri seemed to be following me, so I continued my argument by talking about how the Industrial Revolution changed the world and our approach to retirement.

Back when America was primarily rural, and most folks worked on farms, people continued to work well into their later years. A farmer might need to slow down a bit because of advanced age, but he could continue driving a tractor, overseeing the milking of cows, and contributing to his family's welfare.

That changed forever once machines began dictating the pace of production. Henry Ford's big factory assembly lines couldn't pause for older workers who were "slowing down assembly lines, taking too many personal days and usurping the places of younger, more productive men with families to support."

Some factory bosses tried to pressure older workers into resigning. "The toughest among them refused to quit, even when plant managers turned up the conveyor belts to crazy-fast speeds, like the conveyor belt Charlie Chaplin battled in the movie *Modern Times*." As a result, many older workers were injured or killed on the job.

As younger workers with strong bodies dominated the industrial age, destructive new ideas about **productivity** took root. The basic concept went like this:

*Life is divided into two periods. During the **productive years** people grow, learn, work, and save. Then, during the **nonproductive years,** they get older, see doctors, consume everything they saved, and die.*

I see this destructive idea nearly every day in my retirement counseling work. Men and women equate "work" with "productivity," and see their "working years" as their "productive years." After that, it's all shuffleboard, Winnebago trips, and medical procedures.

I have a radically different approach. I believe people's productive years continue long after their working years. In fact, I've seen how many people actually increased their productivity and their influence *after* leaving jobs and careers that didn't match their passions. Once they left work, that's when their real productivity kicked in because they were doing more of what they were called and gifted to do.

What's Your Plan?

Dave and Terry are similar to most people in one way: They think retirement planning means financial planning. But they're radically different from most people in another way because they've actually spent a good deal of time strategizing together as a couple about their financial situation—both present and future. Most people seem to ignore the subject and ignore planning for it. That's one reason why increasing numbers of people are continuing to work into their 70s and 80s. They feel they have no choice, in part that's because they had no plan, or at least not a sufficient plan.

In a disturbing 2017 report, the Economic Policy Institute said half of all Americans have zero retirement savings. EPI said the vast majority of Americans have less than $1,000 saved.

For years, many workers could rely on their employers—either public or private—to provide pensions in addition to salaries. The idea of public pensions, guaranteed income, started in ancient Rome, but they were restricted to military veterans. In the 19th and 20th centuries, more governments and private companies provided their workers with more benefits, including company-funded retirement plans and government "social security" programs.

But, in recent years, most company funded pension plans have gone away. In the 21st century, many people feel like they are on their own. And some employers seem intent on forcing out older workers. Dave said he could see it happening at his company.

"There are days when I'm feeling increasing pressure at work to 'move on.' I'm not sure why they don't want me around anymore. Is it because they think I cost so much more than a younger manager would cost? Or is my performance on the job really suffering somehow? I think it's probably corporate financial pressure to hire younger workers who would receive lower salaries. Either way, it's discouraging for those of us who have been working for years and are committed to the company."

From Roth to Ruth

Many Americans spend countless hours studying and managing the financial aspects of retirement, like the comparative advantage of standard or Roth IRAs. But few spend much time thinking about the emotional and spiritual aspects of not working. More financial information is a good thing, but it's not the only information we need.

As our lunch time was ending, I pulled out a different source of information, my Bible, to share a few passages with Terri and Dave.

"Our Creator envisions us living lives that are long and full, like it says right here in the Old Testament book of Ruth:

He will renew your life and sustain you in your old age (Ruth 4:15).

The Psalmist also helps us understand God's perspective on living in old age," I said.

The righteous will flourish like a palm tree …
They will still bear fruit in old age,
They will stay fresh and green (Psalm 92: 12-14).

I had one final thought to challenge Terri and Dave.

"A job may be something you can retire from, but work—at least the kind of work I'm talking about—is something that I believe we should continue doing as long as we live."

"I've never heard it explained like that," said Terri. "I will need to think on this for a while!"

"Makes sense to me," said Dave, who agreed to meet with me again a couple of weeks later.

Questions for reflection:

1. Briefly list the 3 key highlights of your work experience or career
   a. ?
   b. ?
   c. ?
2. How did you or were you prepared for your work, career? How much of your preparation was intentional? If so, how?
3. Why is planning for retirement about more than money?
4. What is the role of money in retirement?

CHAPTER 3

THE DREAM OF DOING NOTHING

When Dave met me for lunch a couple of weeks later, he bragged about doing the simple homework assignment I had given him.

"I've got it right here," said Dave, holding two copies of the one-page document he had printed out. "It's my list of the ten things I'm dreaming about doing in retirement."

"Great," I said. "Let's take a look."

Dave and Terri had already done more retirement planning than most folks, but I had surprised them when I told them there was more to retirement planning than financial planning.

"Retirement is so much more than IRAs, 401(k)s, or 403(b)s," I reminded him.

Since our last lunch, Dave had thought long and hard about his plans for retirement. Now he wanted to see how I would react to his list. He handed me a copy and I took a look. I could plainly see that his frustration with work was foremost in his mind.

Dave's Top 10 Retirement Goals

Dave's Top 10 Retirement Goals

(1) Not getting up every morning at 4:30 to open the store at 6:00.

(2) Not driving home every day at 5:00 during crazy rush-hour traffic.

(3) Not having angry customers yell that me.

(4) Not being so worn down by the week's work that weekends are spent resting and recuperating rather than doing the things I want to do, including spending quality time with family.

(5) Not having personal time interrupted by work phone calls, texts, and e-mails.

(6) Not feeling anxious on Sundays about the issues I will confront at work in the coming week.

(7) Not having my time, life, and identity defined by my job.

(8) Not having the energy, or quiet time keeping me from reading a book.

(9) Not spending more years doing what other people tell or expect me to do.

(10) Not measuring my identity or even my success by the titles I have or the money I earn."

"Well," I said. "This is fascinating. You've come up with quite a list here. I can personally identify with everything you wrote down."

"I wasn't sure how the list would come together," said Dave, "but when I sat down and thought about it, all these frustrations just kind of poured out."

"I can see that. Looking at these 10 items, it seems like you're saying you're getting tired of having work and all of its obligations exert such a control over your life."

"Exactly! At times, it seems like there's no *me* anymore, but just this guy who gets up, spends his day working, comes home, and then is too tired and depleted to do anything meaningful."

"I can see that. And I don't think you are alone in feeling that way."

The Lure of "Nothing"

Most people never go through the process Dave did of actually writing down their thoughts about retirement in a numbered list. But the feelings Dave articulates are nearly universal.

The frustrations Dave included on his list are similar to the reactions I hear from many men and women who feel that work has eclipsed pretty much all other areas of their lives. And while I completely understand their frustration, I worry when people try to design multiple decades of life in retirement on the flimsy foundation of "nothing."

Nearly every time I speak to a group or ask an individual about their dreams for retirement, they list more negative items than positive. It seems that many people's dreams for retirement are dominated by their frustrations with their work life rather than their hopes and desires about what they can do once work no longer dominates their daily existence.

Their dreams are about what they are *free from*, not what they are *free to do*.

They are fleeing *from* the burdens of work, not running *to* the many blessings of retirement.

Over the years I have asked thousands of people one simple question about their retirement dreams.

"What are you looking forward to?"

"Doing nothing" is the response I hear more than any other answer.

Over the years I have asked thousands of people one simple question about their dreams for retirement: "What are you looking forward to?" There's a one-word response I hear more than any other answer: "Nothing!"

If you've ever talked to people who are looking forward to retirement, you've probably heard this sentiment yourself. We hear it so often we have come to accept it as normal. After a lifetime of work, the thought a life of "nothing" can seem like a promise of paradise.

Is "Nothing" Enough?

Imagine with me for a moment how you would respond if people in your family or your life gave a similar answer at other key stages of their lives.

Suppose you asked a young child what he wanted to do when he grew up, and instead of saying he wanted to travel to Mars as an astronaut or be the President of the United States, a policeman, fireman or cowboy, he said, "Nothing."

Suppose you asked a recent high school or college graduate what her hopes and plans were, and she said, "Nothing."

Suppose you asked a man in his 30s or 40s who had been laid off from work what he was going to do next, and he said, "Nothing."

Wouldn't you find these answers puzzling or even worrisome?

I understand why Dave is focused on what he *doesn't* want to do once he's no longer working. I understand everything he wants to flee from. We laugh at TV shows like "The Office" and cartoons like "Dilbert" because they make fun of many of the things we hate about work.

But I don't understand why the discussion stops there. I would rather hear people tell me what they *do* want to experience once work no longer dominates their lives. This response comes from those in the non-profit sector as well as secular occupations.

I believe retirement offers people tremendous opportunities: To grow in their faith, to serve God, and to better love their neighbors, all while they enjoy relief from the pressures of work and career.

I have also seen how a future devoted to nothing can lead people to grow frustrated and depressed about the meaninglessness of their lives. Could they actually be doing *something* that brings joy to them and others?

The U-Turn of Unretirement

I told Dave about an interesting trend: A quarter or more of Americans who retire wind up returning to work. These un-retirees include workers, owners, and entrepreneurs who loved their work. They look back with fondness to their working years, but forward to the future with some frustration, or maybe trepidation. For them, retirement promises to rob them of what motivated them.

"I guess it turns out that a life of nothing can be pretty empty and unrewarding," I said, as I reviewed the article with Dave.

New York Times writer Paula Span has been covering America's rapidly aging population in a series called "The New Old Age." In a 2018 article entitled, "When Retirement Doesn't Work Out," Span explored a surprising and growing trend called "unretirement."

The article featured one woman who worked as a nurse and educator for nearly 40 years before retiring. The only "retirement planning" she did was "financial planning," and she did that well. But she failed to plan for *living* in retirement, and three months after retiring she was back at work.

"I'd done all the preparation, except to really think about what life was going to be like," said the woman, who missed the friends and intellectual challenges she experienced every day at work.

Another woman featured in the article unretired after more than a year of retirement. She said not working left her feeling like she was "free-floating" and "very ungrounded."

Back at work at age 69, she has no plans to retire again.

"As long as somebody wants me, I have a lot to contribute."

These two women didn't need to return to work for money. They were seeking other benefits. Cases like theirs explain why economists increasingly talking about *four types of retirement:*

- *Full retirement* = the end of work;
- *Partial retirement* = cutting back work time to fewer hours or days;
- *Delayed retirement* = working into older age to save money for retirement;
- *Unretirement* = returning to work after trying retirement.

People who unretire do so for a variety of reasons. Some miss the social engagement they experience with coworkers. Some feel aimless without regular obligations that force them to get up, get dressed, and get out of the house. Some miss the feeling of accomplishment they experience after achieving goals and meeting challenges at work. The unretirement trend shows that people are struggling to come to terms with the emotional and relational results of retirement.

Seeking More Than Nothing

The growing ranks of the unretired show that "doing nothing" isn't enough for many people. Nothing may be fine for a time, but it's a poor foundation on which to build a meaningful life in retirement.

Longevity expert Robert Hunter proposed a different model that he called "productive aging":

In the 1950's sociologist Ernest Burgess wrote that older people's lives were notably "role less." Little progress has been made since then. Today (2001), the issue takes on new urgency as the average life expectancy rises to 76.6 and evidence suggests a cause-and-effect relationship among health, productivity, and longevity. Studies begun in 1955 by the National Institute of Health have demonstrated that older people who have goals and structure have a better chance of living longer. Thus, health supports productivity and productivity encourages health. Productive aging would appear to be in the best interest of both society and the individual.

Dave talked with me about how he and Terri had done lots of financial planning for retirement, but they had done virtually no "meaning planning."

"You're certainly not alone in that," I said. "Join the crowd! But please don't stay in that spot for long."

I shared with Dave that recent empirical studies found that a felt lack of meaning in retirement is linked to alcohol and drug abuse, depression, anxiety, and suicide. In addition, people who have a purpose in life are better able to cope with losses and life traumas.

"You know," I told Dave, "the Bible has something to say about this contemporary concept of productive retirement. Paul's second letter to the Thessalonians is particularly interesting. Apparently, there were some folks who believed that Jesus was returning right away, so they pretty much decided to lay around and wait for that glorious day. Paul wasn't too excited about that."

I showed Dave the passage:

For you yourselves know how you ought to follow our example. We were not idle when we were with you, nor did we eat anyone's food without paying for it. On the contrary, we worked night and day, laboring and toiling so that we would not be a burden to any of you. We did this, not because we do not have the right to such help, but in order to offer ourselves as a model for you to imitate. For even when we were with you, we gave you this rule: "The one who is unwilling to work shall not eat."

We hear that some among you are idle and disruptive. They are not busy; they are busybodies. Such people we command and urge in the Lord Jesus Christ to settle down and earn the food they eat. And as for you, brothers and sisters, never tire of doing what is good (2 Thessalonians 3:7-13).

"That's what I'm trying to focus on," I said. "Never tiring of doing good, especially not in retirement. I feel there is important work God wants all of us to do. We accomplish some of God's goals at our jobs, but God has other assignments in store for us. Our work continues for a lifetime – during every stage of retirement."

Another Assignment

Dave and I could've talked about retirement and unretirement all day long, but it was already past time for him to rush back to work.

"Can I ask you one more thing, Dave?"

"Sure, fire away!"

"I appreciated the work you did on this assignment about your dreams for retirement, but I'm wondering if you would consider another assignment?"

"OK. What do you want me to think about now?"

"I want you to imagine a time in the future when all of the things you dream about in your list have been removed from your life. You can sleep past 4:30 now. You don't have to endure people yelling at you anymore. All those things are gone.

"What I want you to think about now is one simple question: Now what?

"It's pretty clear what you *don't* want to do with your life. Now we need to figure out what you *do* want to do with your life. Would you mind thinking about that and coming back to me with another list? It doesn't have to be next week, or next month. I want you to think about it for a while."

"Well," said Dave, "that would certainly be an interesting thing to think about!"

"Yes," I answered. "I think it would be *very* interesting!"

Questions for reflection:

1. Are personal goals for retirement different than goals during your working years? If so, How?
2. What do you think about doing "nothing" or "only leisure activities" in Retirement? Why?
3. Are leisure activities the same as doing "nothing", or are they different? Why?
4. Right now, what are your retirement goals? Or, your goals for the next stage of retirement?

CHAPTER 4

A LIFE OF LEISURE

Dave and I met for breakfast two weeks later. Dave was still working on the assignment I had given him the last time we were together, but I had another fun topic we could talk about: Popular ideas about the "perfect" retirement as found in promotional materials for retirement center and communities.

I opened up my manila file folder full of ads I had taken from newspapers and magazines, and as I spread a few of them out over our table at the Omelet Parlor restaurant, Dave grabbed one and pointed at its big, bold headline:

THE GOOD LIFE

"Wow," joked Dave. "I never knew achieving the good life was as simple as moving into the right community!"

"And look at that," I said, pointing at the next line of the ad, which highlighted the community's key selling points:

"Discover a carefree lifestyle where security, relaxation & fun come first."

"That's a mathematical miracle," I said. "Three things can't all be first!"

But as most people realize, the senior living ads I had gathered weren't really designed to provide facts. They were engineered to sell feelings and stoke desires for a lifestyle of leisure, as the first ad's bullet points made perfectly clear:

- *All-Day Restaurant Style Dining*
- *Robust Creative Arts Program*
- *Therapeutic Salt Water Pool.*

Dave grabbed a promotional mailer for a different community that promised residents the moon:

EXPERIENCE LIVING PERFECTED.

"What a deal!" said Dave. "Why be satisfied just living the good life when your life can be perfect?"

"Exactly," I said. "Prior to seeing this ad, I believed that the perfect life was something that only happens to us in heaven."

I picked up a promotional mailer I had received at home promoting a "refined senior community." The mailer didn't include a long list of features or multiple firsts, but instead focused on one thing: food. The mailer highlighted the community's modern restaurant and its celebrity chef as a way of stating the community's marketing distinctive: "Best-in-class amenities and stylish apartment homes."

It had been more than a month since I had met Dave at church. Dave and his wife Terri had just moved to town for Dave's new job. Dave had expressed his frustration with how complex his employer's new retirement plan was, and ever since, we had been meeting to talk about the meaning of retirement.

We decided to talk about "retirement living" this week because both of us had seen so many advertisements selling retirement communities by promising paradise on Earth.

Dave wasn't planning to move into a senior community anytime soon, but the topic interested him because his father, who recently died, had sought "the good life" at a well-known and costly retirement community, only to find that he didn't really enjoy most of the leisure activities it offered.

"It seems like he cut himself off from the people and things he knew," said Dave, "and I always wondered if that was part of what made him become depressed in his final years."

"From what I hear, I think that could be right," I said. "It turns out that a lifetime spent pursuing little more than leisure can be pretty depressing. You can't outsource having a perfect life, or even a good life. That's something you will need to figure out on your own."

Dave was momentarily quiet.

"OK, let's talk about how we got here," I said as I washed down some toast with coffee.

"Great," said Dave, who dug into his omelet. "Sounds interesting."

"Leisure and Recreation for the Active Retired Adult"

I took Dave back in time to January 1, 1960, a major day in modern American retirement history. That was opening day for Sun City, the iconic Arizona retirement community that popularized the concept of building big, new cities around the wants and needs of the growing army of "senior citizens."

"Imagine," I said. "This was a community dedicated to palm trees, golf carts driving down major roads, B. J. Thomas concerts, and restaurant parking lots that fill up by 4 p.m. for senior specials."

I reviewed our discussion from a previous meeting. "Remember that once upon a time, people worked until they died. Even a century or two ago, people quit working because of age or infirmity, and most did not live long after leaving work. All that changed in the 20th century."

We talked about the changes longevity had brought to our society.

"Terri's mom is in her mid-80s," Dave said. "If she stays healthy, she may live another decade or more."

As lifespans grew longer and longer, more people started asking themselves: "OK, what are we going to do with our lives?"

"That's why the idea of retirement communities suddenly made sense," I said.

As lifespans grew longer and longer, there were more people who needed to find a place to live where they could be freed up from having to paint the house, cut the grass, and shovel the snow. This new generation of seniors started asking themselves: "OK, what are we going to do with our lives?"

Sun City answered that question for tens of thousands of residents by pioneering the concept of "building an entire community dedicated to leisure and recreation for the active retired adult."

It was actually typhoid fever that brought Sun City's colorful founder to Arizona. The dry climate proved to be healthy for Del Webb, the successful construction entrepreneur who played golf with and built projects for reclusive billionaire Howard Hughes. He also worked for mobster Benjamin "Bugsy" Siegel to build the Flamingo Hotel and Casino in Las Vegas. (Webb was a supporting character in the 1991 movie, "Bugsy.") A huge baseball fan, he was also a co-owner of the New York Yankees.

Half a century before Sun City, people were already flocking to the warm climes of Florida, where some of the first small retirement communities popped up in the 1920s and 1930s, a period that saw a tripling in the number of American golf courses. In the 1950s, the popularity of television led more people to spend their leisure time being entertained by TV.

Sun City brought all these trends together on a grand scale. Webb had made a huge gamble, but it paid off. More than 100,000 people showed up on opening day to examine the five model homes. Del Webb was featured on the cover of TIME magazine in the summer of 1962 with the headline: "THE RETIREMENT CITY: A New Way of Life for the Old."

As Sun City filled up, Sun City West welcomed the overflow. These two communities house more than 60,000 residents today, and there are additional Sun City locations in Arizona, California, Texas, Nevada, South Carolina, Florida, and outside Chicago.

"I had no idea where this idea came from," said Dave as he leafed through the advertisements in my manila folder.

"How about you?" I asked. "Do you ever see yourself living in a vast retirement community like this?"

"Well," replied Dave after a pause, "hopefully not right away!"

Retirement communities continue to evolve as they respond to the need for intergenerational interaction.

A Good (if not Perfect) Life

Don't get me wrong. I am not trying to demonize Sun City or other retirement communities. They seem to work for many people. My parents lived in Sun City West after my father retired from academia. He had been a Dean of Arts and Humanities at both Arizona State and San Jose State.

I visited my parents there a number of times, and their lives seemed fine. Mom and dad found a good church, a circle of friends with similar interests, and caring neighbors. Dad directed the choir at the local Presbyterian church and mom taught women's classes.

After my father died, I talked to my mom daily about her discussions at the Hole 'n One restaurant, where she often ate breakfast during her last 17 years. Some days it was "the judge" who held court at the table. Other days "the golfer" held her interest. The "gang" as she called them, was her local family.

It was a good life, but I wouldn't quite call it "life perfected." It was more like life abstracted. At times it seemed like I was in a science-fiction movie where a huge spaceship had landed on Earth, scooped up all the seniors from around the U.S., and moved them all to one huge encampment out in the desert.

Everything here revolved around one specific group of people and their needs. It was the opposite of diverse. It was homogenous. The main impression I got from being there was that everything was beige. In this case beige represents not only the colors of things, but also the sameness and homogeneity of all the surroundings. Everything I saw was comfortable and eerily similar.

It was particularly odd to be in a world without children. The sound of a child's voice brings joy to me. To be in a world devoid of that sound seemed as odd as being in a forest without trees.

I remember thinking, "I can see that mom and dad are doing fine, but is this all? Isn't there more?" On one level I was happy for them as they lived out their final years in this trouble-free environment. On the other hand, there was a certain sadness in seeing people seeking to live free of any worries, concerns, or even cold weather. Somehow it seemed to me that God had prepared my parents to do more with their lives during their final years. And their neighbors too!

Bruce Bruinsma

As we saw in the previous chapter, leisure is a beneficial alternative to work. But a life of all work and no play is no good for anyone. When leisure is all there is, and it becomes an end unto itself, it ceases to satisfy. You can only go so far if golf, bridge, and dining out are the focus of your life. I'm concerned that such superficial satisfactions become barriers that keep men and women from discovering the real meaning to life in old age. Simply "going to church" is not a substitute for building the Kingdom.

I was reminded of my visits to Sun City when a disturbing trend caught the nation's attention.

A Crisis of Meaning

A perfect storm of events made suicide front page news in the summer of 2018. Days after celebrated designer Kate Spade and TV tour guide Anthony Bourdain committed suicide, the U. S. Center for Disease Control and Prevention released a starling study.

Deaths by suicide in the country had risen 25% from 1999 to 2016. Nearly 45,000 people died from suicide in 2016. It was not only the young who were dying, but also increasingly those over 65 or 70.

When people experience loss or trauma, it's those who believe life has a purpose who are best able to recover from the stress.

One mental health professional analyzed this trend in a column for *The New York Times*. "I am convinced that our nation's suicide crisis is in part a crisis of meaninglessness," said Clay Routledge, a professor of psychology.

"Empirical studies bear this out … when people experience loss, stress, or trauma, it is those who believe that their lives have a purpose who are best able to cope with and recover from the stress."

Routledge says that deep relationships can help people cope with the stresses they experience in their later years, but superficial relationships aren't strong enough to help. "Merely pleasant or enjoyable social encounters aren't enough to stave off despair," he wrote.

The Mental Health Foundation says one in five retirees experience depression.

24

"People don't realize this," I said, "but there have been some recent studies suggesting that retiring increases a person's chances of suffering from clinical depression by 40 percent."

More to Life

"You know," said Dave. "There are bad times at work when everything seems completely overwhelming. All I can think about at those times is how much I want to get away and enjoy a few hours of fun or recreation. But I couldn't imagine filling years and years of my life with nothing but leisure. That doesn't really seem like much fun!"

"I feel the same way," I said. "Here's one way I look at it. Genesis says we are created in God's image. But what does that mean? I think it means we are created to create. God was a creator, and we were created in His image, so we are supposed to do something, not just sit in an easy chair and watch TV." Our call is to create and bear fruit rather than doing nothing or only leisure.

"Speaking of doing something, I'm supposed to lead a staff meeting in 15 minutes," Dave said. "Let's talk more about that next time, and I promise to finish the assignment you gave me."

Questions for reflection:

1. How does the phrase "meaning and purpose" challenge your thinking? Or does it?
2. Does having identified "meaning and purpose" for your life change anything? If so, how? If not, why not?
3. What is the role of leisure in your retirement plan?
   a. Are you and your spouse on the same page about the role of leisure?
   b. What kind of leisure activities are important to each of you?
4. Can you find a Kingdom building purpose in your leisure pursuits? If so, what is it?
5. What is a good mix of leisure and "meaning and purpose" for you, and for the next decades to come?

CHAPTER 5

THE LONGEVITY REVOLUTION

It had been a while since Dave had showed me his original list of retirement dreams. On that list, all of his dreams were stated negatively. He *didn't* want to get out of bed at 4:30 in the morning anymore. He *didn't* want to be yelled at by angry customers anymore.

I understood his feelings, but I challenged him to think some more about his dream list.

"It's pretty clear what you don't want to do in retirement. The question is: What do you *want* to do?"

Dave had given his dream list further thought, and now he was excited to discuss it with me over lunch.

"Your question challenged me to think about my retirement goals in a completely different way," he said. "I'm still working on my list, but here's my start."

He handed me a brief, one-page document.

Dave's Retirement Goals (version 2.0)

Dave's Retirement Goals (version 2.0)

(1) Taking charge of what I want to do with my hours, my days and my weeks.

(2) Being present and available for Terri, our kids, and future grandkids.

(3) Being more than a "pew sitter" at church and getting involved in a good men's group.

(4) Making a list of books I want to read and movies I want to see and setting aside time to do this.

(5) Exploring options for working or volunteering at something that is meaningful to me.

(6) To be continued...

"Wow, this is completely different from your first list. I like how you are thinking about this."

Dave's new list emphasized a handful of goals he had for the rest of his life after decades spent managing stores around the country for a major home improvement chain.

"You turned your list of don'ts into a list of do's. That's great."

"Yeah," said Dave. "It's easy to gripe about what I don't like at work. It's a little bit more complicated to think through what I really want to do with myself after work no longer dominates my life."

"Exactly, and it's exciting to see your item number five about doing some kind of work or volunteering you. That seems like a conscious choice to do something more than nothing or living a life of leisure."

"Like you said. Nothing may be good for time, but it's no way to live a life. I sure don't want to live my life that way."

"I don't, either. Both of us could be around for another 20 or 30 years. That's a lot of time to spend golfing or playing bridge."

"It sure is."

"As great as this list is, though, there's one thing missing," I said. "Do you think you could find a spot on your list for following God's plan for your life?"

Dave looked at me kind of funny, cocked his head to one side and said,

"Sure. If God has a plan for my future, I better try and figure that out too. That's one plan I would like to line up with." *

We could be around for another 20 or 30 years. That's a lot of time to spend just golfing or playing bridge. And if God has a plan for my future, I better try and figure that out too.

The Supercentenarian

I told Dave about an article I had read about the longest living person in recent human history**. Jeanne Calment was born in Arles, France in 1875, and she lived a quiet life in that city until she became a worldwide celebrity. When she died in 1997, she was 122 years and 164 days old. She outlived her husband, her daughter, and her grandson.

No one is sure why this woman—who met Vincent van Gogh and saw the Eiffel Tower being constructed—lived so long. On the plus side, she walked daily, ate healthy food, and slathered her skin with olive oil. On the other hand, she smoked a few cigarettes a day for nearly 100 years. Her longevity was a likely due to a combination of genes and lifestyle. [1]

Some elderly people worry about where they will find the money to live, but Calment benefited from a great real estate deal that became a financial lifeline. In 1965, a French man agreed to purchase her home and pay her a monthly sum until she died, at which point he would own her apartment, his presumption was that she had only a short time to live. She left the house to enter a retirement home when she was 110, meaning he paid her this monthly sum for more than three decades. Not all assumptions are true.

Few people can expect to live as long as Calment did. I know many people who hope and pray they *don't* live that long. But while she is an outlier, we humans are living longer and longer than we ever have, which means we will spend more years in retirement than previous generations. Recent genetic research suggests 120 as a reasonable longevity expectation.

---

[1] * See John 16:15
** See Genesis 5:27

Is Ninety the New Seventy?

Human life expectancy has grown longer over the years, even though there are regular tragedies that interrupt the statistical progress, including wars, plagues, diseases like AIDS, natural disasters, and human-caused disasters like the opioid epidemic. (More than 100 Americans die every day from overdosing on opioids.) While these impact the average, your longevity may not be impacted by them.

Our ancient Stone Age ancestors could expect to live an average of 20 years or so. The native people who lived in the southern United States and Latin America in the centuries before the arrival of Christopher Columbus could expect to live 20 to 30 years. By the 18th and 19th centuries, people in England averaged 40 years of life.

But in the last century, the world's average life expectancy rate has skyrocketed:

- From 31 years (in 1900);
- To 48 years (in 1950);
- To 71 years (in 2014)
- If you do live to age 65, your life expectancy rises to the mid-80's and extends to 104.

Advances in medicine, sanitation and diet have helped extend human lives, but there are still big differences between haves and have-nots. In the U.S., life expectancy is 79.68 years, which ranks as #43 in the list of countries with the longest life expectancies. Number one is Monaco, at 89.52 years. Number 224 is Chad, at 49.81 years.

No matter how you slice it, people are living much longer. We may not live as long as Jeanne Calment, but many of us will spend 20-30 years in retirement. What a long time to waste, and what a wonderful opportunity to do something amazing in these valuable decades of life.

Longer Lives: Two Views

Dave seemed pleased to learn about longer life spans.

"I'm starting to think about some of the ways I can best use all the time, multiple decades and life stages I may have. I know I want to enjoy life in retirement, but I want to make sure I invest time in the things I wrote down on my new retirement dream list. These things are important to me."

"I feel the same way," I replied. "I want to make the most of every day. But not everybody feels that way."

"What do you mean?"

"I talk to people every day who take a much dimmer view. As they see it, there's nothing ahead but a long, slow slog through health issues, cognitive problems, and finally death. They look to the future and seem themselves living in a series of less and less welcoming residences as they transition from independent living at home, to an assisted living center, to a nursing homes with medical facilities, to hospice, to a cemetery." This seems to be the overall view of our culture.

It seems that the people who talk about aging as a "long slow slog" often focus on preserving their physical and mental health instead of learning or trying new things. The people who view their later years as an opportunity to live, grow, experiment, and make new discoveries are typically more excited about what the future holds.

"In the end, we can't control how long we will live. We can only control how we will live. That's what Judy has done."

I told Dave about how I see my wife Judy as a good example of living with gusto and trying new things. At age 58 she decided to try something completely different: She became a flight attendant for American Airlines. Initially, Judy was concerned that she might not be able to keep up with her fellow trainees, most of whom were in their 20s. But by the time the six-week training regimen was completed, many of these younger trainees had flunked out. Some were unable to adjust their body clocks to the unusual training schedule, which started at 4 a.m. on some days, and at 1 p.m. on other days. (The schedule was designed to mirror flight attendants' daily work assignments, which differ from day to day.)

Judy was able to wake up both her body and her brain, no matter what time of day it was. And for the next ten years she was excited every day to learn new things about people and let her light shine in the skies before thousands of people she never would have otherwise met.

The Longevity Premium

Whenever people start telling me that living in retirement will be a long, slow slog, I present a different vision. It's something I call the Longevity Premium. We will explore this longevity premium in full in Chapter 8. Meanwhile, here's my one sentence summary:

Much like a good wine, a good life gets better with age.

While it is true that many people experience physical and cognitive problems as they grow older, old-age also brings unique benefits that are unavailable to people with fewer years under their belts.

The Longevity Premium means old age brings benefits. Much like a good wine, a good life gets better with age.

Wisdom is one part of the longevity premium. People say experience is the best teacher, and by the time we reach our 50s and 60s, life experience has taught us a great deal. I believe wisdom actually accelerates with age. Older doesn't always make wiser, but it's typically the case. Years' worth of experience and intellectual growth bring a greater ability to have perspective and providing the foundation for making important decisions.

Another important part of the longevity premium is spiritual and personal growth. People who spent decades immersed in work and family responsibilities find greater opportunities for connecting with God and serving people after some of these responsibilities fall away or lighten up.

Retirement by itself does not suddenly make people more spiritual, but people in their 50s and 60s often tell me that they find themselves giving more time and energy to prayer, Bible study, meditation, reflection, and service to others than they ever did during their go-go years when they were managing families and careers.

I asked Dave if he had seen any evidence of these spiritual changes in his own life as he grew older.

"I thought it was interesting that your new list of retirement goals includes a couple of items that are on my own list. You talked about getting more involved with church and a men's group, and you said you wanted to spend more time reading books. I found these items interesting because

I've seen that as people age, many become more intentional about their spiritual and intellectual lives. Suddenly, they have opportunities to grow and explore what wasn't open to them earlier in life."

"That sounds pretty good," said Dave. "But right now, everything in my life seems to be moving too fast for any sustained reflection of any kind! When I try to sit down for a few minutes to pray or read, and my mind just spins out of control about all the things I need to take care of. I'm really looking forward to finding more time and space to just be quiet, think, and pray without having my 'To Do' list dominate my mind."

"I can see that. And I guess another joy of growing older is being able to exert more control over my 'To-Do' list. Now I have more chances to do the things that are most important, not just the many things that seem so urgent."

"That sounds like something to look forward to," said Dave.

Moses and St. Patrick: Preparation for Service

When I talk to groups about having a more intentional view of retirement, I often talk about Moses, the man the Book of Deuteronomy calls "the man of God" because he heard God's call, led his people out of bondage in Egypt, and received the Ten Commandments from God on a mountaintop.

But Moses wasn't born with deep faith and a passion for serving God. He learned these things through a long life that was filled with challenge and heartbreak. I look at Moses' long life through the prism of preparation. His early years and young adulthood prepared him for the work God would later call him to take on.

Born At a time when the Israelites were an oppressed minority that was exploited by the Egyptian Pharaoh, he escaped death as an infant when his mother hid him to protect him from Pharaohs order to kill Israelite boys. He was found and rescued by Pharaoh's daughter, allowing him to learn the ways of the Egyptian court.

After seeing an Egyptian slave master abusing Israelite slaves, he killed the slave master, forcing him to flee Egypt.

40 years later, God would send Moses back to Egypt for a larger

purpose: releasing the Israelites from slavery. God called Moses to do the job, and even though he was a poor speaker who needed his brother Aaron to handle his public communication, Moses shouldered the assignment and led his people to freedom.

Many centuries later, a similar kind of preparation would enable St. Patrick to effectively evangelize Ireland in the fifth century. Patrick grew up in England but was abducted by Irish pirates who sold him as a slave. Patrick worked many years as a shepherd, learning much about Ireland's culture, customs, and pagan Celtic belief system.

When he finally had a chance, Patrick escaped back to England, enjoying his family and his freedom once again. But wouldn't you know it? That's when God called him to return to Ireland as his servant. Patrick accepted God's call and launched a new chapter of his life. Now Patrick would show the Celts how to devote themselves to the one true God, not their old pagan gods.

Each and every life is unique. God has strengthened you with experiences and wisdom that no one else has experienced. Just think of all the amazing ways God can put those things to use for his bigger purposes, if only you will listen for his call and faithfully follow it.

A New Beginning

Dave and I were talking about Moses and Patrick when he looked at his watch.

"Oops, I've got to go back to work now and 'serve my master.' But maybe someday soon I will be but in a better position to serve God."

"I think you will," I said. "I think you will."

"That sounds good."

"You know, God doesn't just call us once in life. He calls us again and again. We need to be listening and ready to respond."

"My ears are wide open!"

"By the way, I will be leading a 'Reframing Retirement' series at church in a couple of months. Is that something you and Terri might like to attend?"

"That sounds like something we will definitely check out," said Dave.

Questions for reflection:

1. Why is it important to understand the reality of longevity?
2. What are some key benefits of longevity?
3. What new challenges are created by longevity?
4. Based on your health and family history, as you know it, how long do you expect to live?

SECTION 2

THE RETIREMENT REFORMATION:
CHANGING HOW WE SEE
THE SEASONS OF LIFE

CHAPTER 6

FAITHFUL FOR A LIFETIME: A PERSONAL JOURNEY

There are around 800,000 words in the Bible, but two of the most powerful words stand out in the four Gospels: "Follow me."

We first hear this powerful invitation when Jesus called Peter and Andrew:

As Jesus was walking beside the Sea of Galilee, he saw two brothers, Simon called Peter and his brother Andrew. They were casting a net into the lake, for they were fishermen. "Come, follow me," Jesus said, "and I will send you out to fish for people." At once they left their nets and followed him (Matthew 4:18-20).

Next up was Matthew: *As Jesus went on from there, he saw a man named Matthew sitting at the tax collector's booth. "Follow me," he told him, and Matthew got up and followed him* (Matthew 9:9).

Jesus issued the same call to a rich man he met one day, but that man rejected His invitation:

Jesus answered, "If you want to be perfect, go, sell your possessions and give to the poor, and you will have treasure in heaven. Then come, follow me."

When the young man heard this, he went away sad, because he had great wealth. (Matthew 19:21).

Jesus issued this simple call many times in the Gospels. But these invitations did not cease after His crucifixion. After his resurrection, Jesus continued to call men and women to follow Him and be His disciples. The Holy Spirit is a consistent voice for us to hear.

Jesus still calls men and women to follow Him today. I am grateful to be one of the people who heard His call many years ago and chose to follow him.

But hearing Christ's call is not a one-time event. We must seek His voice and listen for His guidance again and again, day after day, moment by moment. That guidance often comes in surprising ways, as I saw a few years ago when I met two veteran missionaries named Bill and Betty.

Hearing Christ's call is not a one-time event. We must seek His voice and listen for His guidance again and again, day after day, moment by moment.

Are You Ready?

In 1988, I got a phone call from Ronald, a long-time friend who gives financial support to missionaries around the world.

"I've been helping two devoted missionaries for 28 years, and they're hoping to retire in a couple of years," Ronald told me. "They say they are ready and prepared, but I'm not so sure. Can you meet with them and help them figure this out?"

I agreed to meet with them, not realizing they would help me much more than I helped them. We met in my office on a rainy Thursday evening.

"We love serving the Lord in Africa, but we are getting older, and it's time for us to come back to America so settle into a new life and be closer to our grandchildren," Bill told me.

"Our mission agency has been paying into a retirement plan for us for the past 20 years," said Betty, "and we're relying on that. I probably want to retire sooner than Bill does."

"Wow," I said. "That's impressive that your agency has been so committed over so long a time to funding your retirement. That's not always the case."

"Yes," said Betty. "We've heard horror stories about missionaries who worked for decades and decided to retire, only to find out they couldn't.

That's why we were so happy our agency regularly made this contribution to a nest egg for us."

"That's great," I said. "Can you tell me a little bit about your plan?"

Bill handed me a folder full of papers that he had been clutching in his hands. I hurriedly looked through the papers, piecing together a picture of their retirement funding. My stomach sank when I saw information about their pension, which was a defined benefit plan.

"OK, it looks like your retirement plan will yield you $13 of retirement pay per month for every year of service," I said, reaching for my trusty calculator. I already knew the answer, but I was stalling for time.

"OK, that works out to $364 of retirement income per month."

No one said a word, but the look on Bill's face screamed disbelief and betrayal.

"$364?" he confirmed.

"I'm sorry to have to say this, but if this is your plan, I have some bad news for you. You aren't ready to retire in a couple of years. I'm afraid you're not even close."

This wasn't the first time I had delivered depressing news to people who thought they were financially prepared for retirement but lacked the necessary financial resources. But Bill and Betty's case broke my heart. Two humble servants who devoted their lives to serving God had trusted their mission agency to care for their retirement. Now felt that trust had been misplaced, and that they should have performed their own calculations earlier.

Betty started crying quietly.

"I don't know what to say," she said, dabbing at her eyes with a Kleenex. "We hoped that this would take care of us. We believed there would be enough."

"So," said Bill, after taking a minute to let everything sink in. "What do we do now?"

From Anger to Action

I told Bill and Betty that I would do what I could to help them, and we stayed in touch for the next seven years. After wrapping up their service in

Africa, they came back to the U.S. to work at the mission agency's offices, so they could generate more income and put away some savings.

They worked seven years in that office to get their financial house in order. Their scenario reminded me of the biblical story of Jacob and Laban. Jacob wanted to marry Rachel, but her shrewd father Laban got seven years of work out of Jacob before letting him marry her.

Working for seven more years was the best solution anybody could come up with to address the financial shortfall Bill and Betty faced, but I wasn't going to forget about this disturbing episode any time soon. I didn't realize it at the time, but my work with Bill and Betty would soon change the course of their lives—and mine.

I was angry to see two of God's faithful servants in this difficult situation. I was frustrated with the neglect and poor planning that had led them to my office. I was saddened that God's servants had been misled into believing that they would be taken care of in their later years. My friend Ronald was equally upset. He had never known anything about this problem during all the years he supported Bill and Betty and many other missionaries.

I discovered long ago that when I get angry and frustrated, my emotions rarely change the problem that caused me to be upset. These feelings raise my blood pressure, but they don't do anything to address the issues that caused the problem.

This time I turned my anger into action. I decided to roll up my sleeves and dive in. My goal was to do something that would help missionaries around the world think ahead and be better prepared for retirement when their work on the field was done.

All my conversations with Bill and Betty and other missionaries happened in the U.S. when they came back on furlough, doing church visitations, and raising money. But I felt it would be better to talk to missionaries about their lives and their retirement dreams on their own turf. I believed they would be better served if our planning discussions were held on the field where they worked, not back in Birmingham or Pasadena.

I called the head of one mission agency again and told him my idea. We set up a meeting for the following week in his office.

Will You Follow Me All the Way to Timbuktu?

I explained my experience with Bill and Betty to the mission leader. "I do want to help these people think about their preparation—or lack of preparation—for retirement. But I really believe I need to have these conversations with them *over there*, not here in the U.S. while they're busy visiting churches and supporters."

"That makes a lot of sense," the executive said.

"Well," I asked, "how can I figure this out?"

He got up from his desk, walked to a huge world map that covered one of the walls of his office, and pointed to a spot on the map.

"Here," he said. "This is where you should go. You can figure it out there."

I got up from my seat and walked over to the map so I could see where his finger was pointing. His index finger was in western Africa. I could read the name of the country: M-A- L-I. I had never heard of Mali before, and until now I had no idea where it was located.

Then I focused on the name of the city where his finger was resting. I saw the name: T-I-M-B-U-K-T-U.

I had certainly heard of Timbuktu before, but more as a metaphor for the end of the world, than an actual place. All I could think of was how somebody would say, "Well, such and such a place is as far away as Timbuktu."

"You're joking," I said to my friend. "You don't literally want me to go to Timbuktu, do you?"

"Actually, yes," he said. "We have two missionary couples there who are approaching retirement age. "Unfortunately, there are no good road routes, but we can get you there on a small missionary plane from the capitol city of Bamako."

My head was reeling. Sure, I wanted to help missionaries, but I had no idea I would begin this new work by traveling around the world to a place that was famous for its remoteness and inaccessibility. Literally I was being sent to the end of the world. The story of Jonah flashed through my mind.

What is this guy thinking? I asked myself. The answer I got stunned me.

"Follow me," I heard a voice say.

I looked at Jonathan, but he wasn't talking. I told him I would think and pray about it and get back to him soon. It was Jesus talking to me. He was asking me to follow Him once again, but if I accepted this invitation it would take me all the way to you-know-where.

I wrestled like crazy for a few days over how to make the right decision. I also did a little research. The ancient city of Timbuktu, founded over 1,000 years ago, was an important center of learning and trade in gold and salt. Then came centuries of decline. (In more recent years, the city has been plagued by various Islamic terrorist groups.)

I was interested, but also skeptical. Why would anybody spend their own time, money, and energy to do something like this?

Then I heard the voice again. "Follow me."

I talked to Judy and explained everything that had happened with the missionaries and the map and Timbuktu and Jesus calling. She surprised me by looking me straight in the eyes and saying, "You're actually going to go and do this, aren't you?"

It was all the confirmation I needed. Timbuktu here I come.

Obeying the Call

I was uncertain and even a bit afraid as I made my plans to travel to a remote spot on the other side of the world, but I had no choice. It seemed like God had given me a challenge I couldn't refuse:

Okay, Bruce, you talk a good game about how concerned you are about missionaries and my many servants around the world. But are you willing to risk stepping out of your privileged American comfort zone for three weeks to actually experience the difficult conditions some of these servants deal with every day of their lives as you talk to them about their long-term plans.

I thought about how Jesus had called his disciples—one by one—to follow Him. Now it was like Jesus was saying, *Bruce, will you follow Me wherever I take you?*

I was undergoing a mid-life gut-check. As a teen I had accepted Jesus as my savior. As a young man, I came to acknowledge Christ's lordship over my life. I sought to serve him as I made decisions about the work I would do, who I would marry, and other major decisions. But it had been a while since I had faced a test like this one: If God called me to do something, would I actually do it?

I was undergoing a mid-life gut-check. If God called me to do something, would I actually do it?

I went to Timbuktu. It was a rough trip, but it was also amazing. I saw a side of the world and a devotion to Christian service I had never seen before. Sitting together in 130-degree heat, we talked about God's plans for their future, financial preparation, and what it means to return to what has become a foreign culture, home. An ancient mosque built with mud bricks, voodoo drums at midnight and flying over miles of endless desert, are all special memories.

After I came back, I looked at things in new ways. Suddenly everything became clear. Now I understood why God had been calling me to follow him once again. Because I had gone, I felt I had "passed the test." Now He wanted me to help care for his servants, the men and women who were busy sowing the precious seeds of salvation that His parable of the sower taught about.

Soon, God began bringing new opportunities my way that allowed me to change the course of my work and my career. a few months after I got back from Mali, I received another interesting phone call from an executive with a major Christian denomination that supports thousands of missionaries around the world.

"I hear you traveled all the way to Timbuktu to help missionaries prepare for retirement," he said. "Would you be willing to travel a much shorter distance—to our main office in the U.S.—to meet with me and other denominational leaders so we can discuss ways we can better care for our missionaries?"

I gladly accepted the invitation to work with the denominational executives, helping them put together new retirement plans for their missionaries so none of them would experience the problems Bill and Betty faced.

Before I knew it, I was charted a new course for my life. Word spread about what I was doing, and the calls kept coming in. I also called ministry leaders I knew and told them what I was doing. Many of them asked me, "Will you help us, too?"

Then my daughter Bethany got involved.

"I've seen all the missionaries who are coming to see you," she said.

"That's great. But what about pastors? I don't know if you realize it, but many pastors face their own difficult retirement problems. Is there anything we can do for them?"

Initially, I was skeptical. Bethany's proposal seemed like it was going in a different direction from my calling to help missionaries. But the more I thought about it, it became clearer. I would help all of God's servants plan and prepare for the future.

Looking back 30 years later, I thank God for changing my life and my career through this whole experience. Age brings perspective, and I can now see how one conversation with two missionaries, along with one trip to the "uttermost parts of the earth," set in motion a series of events that I did not see coming:

- Within 18 months of visiting Timbuktu, Bethany[2] and I started an organization called the Christian Retirement Coalition to serve missionaries and pastors.
- Years later, we changed the name to Envoy Financial. According to Proverbs, an envoy is a trusted messenger. Bethany and I managed Envoy together from 1991-2018.
- Today, Envoy serves some 4,000 churches, almost 200 Christian non-profit organizations, thousands of pastors and a large number of missionaries around the world.

"Is It You, Lord?"

I'm telling you this history to highlight my journey. I want you to see me as an example of what I am saying throughout this book: God has work for all of us to do, and that work doesn't stop when we hit the age of 60, or 70, or even 80. As long as we continue listening and following, God continues to call us.

My experience with the missionaries reminds me of the Old Testament

---

[2] Bethany Palmer is Bruce and Judy Bruinsma's daughter and was a partner at Envoy Financial for over 20 years. Bethany then joined her husband Scott in creating The 5 Money Personalities.

passage where God calls Samuel. This curious passage shows that it's not always easy to hear God's call:

The boy Samuel ministered before the LORD *under Eli. In those days the word of the* LORD *was rare; there were not many visions.*

One night Eli, whose eyes were becoming so weak that he could barely see, was lying down in his usual place. The lamp of God had not yet gone out, and Samuel was lying down in the house of the LORD, *where the ark of God was.*

Then the LORD *called Samuel. Samuel answered, "Here I am." And he ran to Eli and said, "Here I am; you called me."*

But Eli said, "I did not call; go back and lie down." So, he went and lay down.

Again, the LORD *called, "Samuel!" And Samuel got up and went to Eli and said, "Here I am; you called me."*

"My son," Eli said, "I did not call; go back and lie down."

Now Samuel did not yet know the LORD: *The word of the* LORD *had not yet been revealed to him.*

A third time the LORD *called, "Samuel!" And Samuel got up and went to Eli and said, "Here I am; you called me."*

Then Eli realized that the LORD *was calling the boy. So, Eli told Samuel, "Go and lie down, and if he calls you, say, 'Speak,* LORD, *for your servant is listening.'" So, Samuel went and lay down in his place.*

The LORD *came and stood there, calling as at the other times, "Samuel! Samuel!" Then Samuel said, "Speak, for your servant is listening."*

And the LORD *said to Samuel: "See, I am about to do something in Israel that will make the ears of everyone who hears about it tingle* (1 Samuel 3: 1-11).

Three times God called Samuel, and three times Samuel failed to realize it was God speaking to him. Has the same thing ever happened to you?

As I talk to people who are approaching or already living in retirement, I see many of these older and largely inactive believers as "dormant Christians." They love God but they're not actively seeking (and maybe not even open to) hearing God's call to embrace another divine assignment.

God is still calling, but many seniors often fill their lives with "nothing" or leisure, unaware that God is still enlisting their help in building his kingdom. Our response to God's call should not be to ignore it. It's time to listen.

Some people say God mostly calls us when we are young, but I don't think that's the case. I believe God calls us to follow him in new ways at various times throughout our lives, even in our 60s, 70s, 80s, and even our 90s.

What Is God Calling You to Be and Do?

The older I get, the more I appreciate the ways God has guided and used me in the past, and the more I seek to hear his voice in the future. As I've studied scripture and Christian biographies, and talked to people around the world, I've discovered that God seems to want his older servants to focus on four main goals.

1) Being faithful for a lifetime.

When I was growing up, most people worked until they retired at 65, and many died at 67 or 68. If you lived into your 70's, you were considered *really* old.

Now people experience 10, 20 or even 30 years of retirement. So, what do we do with all this time we have left? I believe these additional years give us even more time to love God, love our neighbor, and be faithful to our calling for a lifetime, not just a season.

So, what does being faithful for a lifetime look like? In my experience, the process often happens like this:

- First, God chooses His servants for a purpose. (We will explore finding your purpose and calling in Chapter 13.)
- He then calls us to a task and role in building His Kingdom here on earth.
- Then he strengthens us for the tasks He has given us.
- Finally, he upholds us when we are weak, failing, or confused.

These are just a few of the great promises of God that give us strength for the day and perseverance to finish our tasks. Our goals and plans should revolve around God's plan for our lives as we seek to faithfully do His will. It is easy to nod and agree. It's a little harder to actually follow.

If we can learn to be faithful for a lifetime, we will impact the world by planting mustard seeds that grow really big. We will play a role in building God's kingdom when we follow Him faithfully.

2) Seeking Gods direction.

Thirty years ago, when God sent me to Timbuktu, I was hungry for God's will and guidance in my life. He used that willingness on my part to advance his Kingdom objectives.

What about you? When is the last time you asked God to guide you and use you for His glory? Was it when you were seeking guidance over your career or a choice of mate?

If so, it's time for you to open the conversation again and let God know you're still available for service. You might be surprised and thrilled to see what He wants you to do next. You might not go to Timbuktu, but He has *something* for you to do *somewhere*.

Our mature years are a great opportunity to fulfill the Psalmist's plea: "Be still and know that I am God" (Psalm 46:10). Listening to God's whisper starts with our willingness to be still. In the cacophony of life, it is increasingly hard to do. Each of us has a special listening place. It is important we find it, use it, and listen to God.

3) Letting Faith Grow into Faithful Action.

God has graciously redeemed us. But redemption is not the end of the road. It's merely the preface for our new roads as God-followers, as Paul pointed out:

For it is by grace you have been saved, through faith—and this is not from yourselves, it is the gift of God—not by works, so that no one can boast. For we are God's handiwork, created in Christ Jesus to do good works, which God prepared in advance for us to do (Ephesians 2:8-10).

I believe there are people and places in our world that desperately need you, your wisdom, your talents, your experience, your hands, your heart and yes, your energy. Allow God to send you and use you in new and exciting ways and you will see how He has prepared you for service without your even knowing it.

4) Living and Serving from a Loving Posture.

For the Old Testament Israelites, the goal in life was to praise and serve God while following the rules he laid down in the Ten Commandments and the Mosaic law.

Then Jesus came along and basically said, "I'm replacing all the old rules. I want you to love God and love your neighbor. This is the "first and greatest commandment" Jesus spoke about in Matthew 22:38.

Earlier I talked about how angry I was when I learned that Bill and Betty would not be able to retire any time soon, regardless of what they had been led to believe. But anger makes a poor fuel, and over the years I have achieved more with my love than I have with my anger.

Paul explains the importance of love in his famous love chapter:

If I speak in the tongues of men or of angels, but do not have love, I am only a resounding gong or a clanging cymbal. If I have the gift of prophecy and can fathom all mysteries and all knowledge, and if I have a faith that can move mountains, but do not have love, I am nothing. If I give all I possess to the poor and give over my body to hardship that I may boast, but do not have love, I gain nothing (1 Corinthians 13:1-3).

The longer I follow Christ, the more I see His love living within me. I'm not creating this love, I'm merely receiving it and passing it on to others. I am following my master's command: "This is my command: Love each other" (John 15:17).

Whatever God calls you to do, please remember to do it in love.

God Is Calling. Are You Listening?

God calls all His children to love Him and serve Him. If you haven't been hearing His call, it's not because He has gone mute or stopped talking. Maybe it's you. Maybe you need to actively seek His will and listen.

Unfortunately, it often seems that many people have retired from hearing God's call for their lives. As the population of older Americans grows larger and larger, this trend is turning us into the largest underutilized group in His entire church family.

When I stand before Christ at the final judgment, I don't want the report to come back that I was AWOL the last third of my life. I would much rather hear Him say: "Well done, good and faithful servant! You have been faithful with a few things; I will put you in charge of many things. Come and share your master's happiness!" (Matthew 25:21).

God is still calling us. He still has much for you to do.

Are you listening?

Are you ready to serve?

God called me to go to Timbuktu. I believe He's calling all seniors to follow Him in retirement.

Many people see retirement as "freedom from" something, and that something is typically work and all its attendant demands and restrictions.

I'm inviting you to see retirement as a "freedom to," not a "freedom from." In retirement, we have a freedom to follow God and serve our neighbors that we never had before. Let's make the best use of this incredible gift.

That's what it means to be faithful for a lifetime.

Questions for Reflection

1) When has God used me?

Think back over the many years and seasons of your life. Are there some periods where you can say, "Wow, I can really see how God used me in that season."?

Now think back over the last 10 to 20 years of your life. How has God used to during this season?

2) Are you seeking God's will for your life?

What do you say when you pray to God? Hopefully, you thank Him for His goodness and praise Him for who He is. But do you also ask Him to guide you into ways you can serve Him? If not, try adding this request to your normal daily prayers, and see what happens.

3) Are you willing to follow him?

"Follow me," Jesus told His disciples. He issues the same invitation to us today, just as He did with me when I went to Timbuktu. Are you willing to follow Christ anew in this season of your life?

Questions for reflection:

1. What does the term, "Faithful for a lifetime" mean to you? How long is a lifetime to you?
2. List three key times of transition in your life, and what you learned from each one
   a. ?
   b. ?
   c. ?
3. How have you heard God's call on your life?
   a. If so, how?
   b. If not, do you think there is one? Or more?
4. Does the idea of a change in your thinking about retirement, a Retirement Reformation, make sense to you?
   a. If so why?
   b. If not, why not?

CHAPTER 7

IT'S COMPLICATED: THE 6 RETIREMENT QUESTIONS YOU CAN'T IGNORE

Jim and Lara have been married for more than 30 years, and both know that retirement is sneaking up on them and getting closer year-by-year. But in all their time together they've never had a serious, sustained, successful conversation on the topic of their long-term future.

Most of the time, retirement comes up only when something happens at work that makes Jim want to retire sooner, or when Lara sees something in a news broadcast or magazine that stimulates her thinking.

This time, it was an article in *Field & Stream* magazine that led Jim to mention retirement at around 7:30 one Tuesday evening as the two of them were in their family room reading magazines and watching TV.

"This is it," he said, pointing at an article about a small retirement community on Idaho's Salmon River that was designed for people who love fishing. "*This* is what I would love to do."

"Well," said Lara, "I would rather move to Mississippi so we can be closer to the grandchildren."

Thus, ended Jim and Lara's latest unsuccessful conversation about retirement.

They're not alone. As we showed in Chapter 2, many people do *financial planning* for retirement, but most fail to *plan how they will live* in retirement. Many look forward simply to "doing nothing" after they leave work. Their focus is *freedom from* something—typically work—not *freedom to do* something.

Most people expect that retirement will usher in a period of ease and relaxation. Jim, who has worked for decades as an accountant, looks forward to a time when he can rest his tired brain from all the calculations and decision-making that are a daily part of his job.

But I have news for Jim and for anyone else who imagines retirement to be some kind of mindless nirvana. The reality couldn't be more different. Retirement is complicated, and in many ways it's more complicated than life before retirement. I know that's counterintuitive, and perhaps also frustrating, but it's true.

I've talked to many couples who see retirement as if it's one of those big, 3,000-piece puzzles that can cover a table top. They can see how the puzzle *should* look by looking at the photo on the box, but they're overwhelmed by all the tiny pieces and don't know how to start putting them all together, so they create a coherent, sustained vision of God's plan for their lives.

Retirement offers people opportunities to do things differently than they have before but taking advantage of those opportunities requires choices and decision making. Suddenly, people come to a fork in their road and need to determine which way they will go. Decisions must be made that will be life-changing for years to come.

If you want your transition to retirement to go smoothly and your experience in retirement to be positive, you are going to need to think long and hard about your goals, passions, and priorities.

There are six major questions you need to answer as you prepare to head into retirement:

1) How are we going to relate to each other?
2) What are we going to do?
3) Where are we going to do it?
4) Who are we going to do it with?
5) How are we going to finance it?
6. What is most important in retirement?

We will devote the rest of this chapter to unpacking these key questions, regardless whether you are married or single, younger or older, wealthy or poor.

1) How are we going to relate to each other?

In a sense, Jim and Lara are better off than some couples. True, they appear to have significant differences in their retirement dreams. He prefers Idaho and she prefers Mississippi. But at least for now they seem willing to stick it out with each other as they figure out what they're going to do.

Other couples aren't so lucky. When they reach retirement age, their marriages totally fall apart. That's why social scientists are talking about a disturbing trend that I'm seeing play out all over the country: gray divorce.

Gray divorce is the term used for divorce by people who are 50 or older, which is increasingly common. The Pew Research Center described the problem in a 2017 report entitled: "Led by Baby Boomers, divorce rates climb for America's 50+ population." The report concluded: "Among U.S. adults ages 50 and older, the divorce rate has roughly doubled since the 1990s."

Couples who "stayed together because of the children" often see no need to stay together once the children are gone, and they probably won't stay together unless they can get together and envision a new kind of friendship, a renewed friendship, that will take them through the years to come.

There are many powerful factors that cause marriages to unravel in retirement. Let me describe just a few:

New and Unusual Feelings.

When a person who has worked steadily for decades quits working, all kinds of emotional and intellectual changes take place.

Initially, many experience relief or even euphoria at their newfound freedom, but in time these positive feelings can be replaced by anxiety, dread, and remorse.

Many retirees tell me they feel a sense of emptiness and purposelessness after walking away from their jobs and the people they have worked with for years.

"Work was hard," one retired executive told me, "but at least when I worked, I felt important, valued, and respected. Now that I no longer have that professional identity, I feel like a big nobody."

Others tell me they feel lost, confused, detached, directionless, stressed, anxious, useless, oblivious, or lonely. It's like John Prine sang in the chorus of his popular 1971 song, "Hello in There":

Old people just grow lonesome
Waiting for someone to say, "Hello in there, hello."

These powerful feelings can be confusing and disorienting, and they can cause a disturbing distance to grow between men and women who don't know how to talk together about their feelings—including their feelings about the future.

Long-simmering issues or resentments.

When Lara told Jim, she preferred Mississippi over Idaho, she was expressing frustrations that had built up in her over decades as the couple moved from city to city to accommodate Jim's career. She hadn't previously expressed these sentiments to Jim, but now they were rising to the surface as she realized retirement was looming.

"I followed him wherever he went for as long as we have been married," she said. "Now I would like him to follow me for a change."

Even the simplest discussions can shift to a battle over issues of power, equality, and priority. I have talked to shocked and frightened husbands who say their wives suddenly want to have greater say in their decisions. One even said his wife had turned into a "flaming feminist."

A man told me a conversation with his wife about what they would do in retirement led to this angry rebuttal:

"You are not going to ignore me and my needs and my desires any longer. Now it's time for me to have my say, and you're going to come along with me on this one instead of me following you all the time."

For some couples, retirement opens up new opportunities to spend time together and deepen their relationship, but for others, retirement seems to raise old issues that make divorce look like a viable choice. Moms and dads now living in "empty nest" with no children to distract them need to find new ways to relate to each other and love and respect one another.

I typically counsel couples to avoid divorce because of the havoc it will play on their retirement savings and financial futures—as well as their families. But in some cases, too much damage has been done, and after a life of struggle, work, and raising kids, many married men and women decide to go their separate ways and try something new in the years they have left. Unfortunately, many people find that their new marriages have just as many problems as their previous marriages—but with different players. We don't leave our problems and issues, we just drag them along.

People often ask Judy and I to tell the secret of our nearly 60-year marriage. Our answers are simple.

1) We made a commitment not to divorce, and we kept that commitment. We figured that if God had truly brought us together, it's unlikely He would now be taking us apart from each other. Our union is strong, though it has faced challenges, hard decisions, and gut-wrenching realities. How have we stayed married? We did not get divorced. Sometimes, it's just that simple.

2) We have followed Jesus' command to love one another and have worked hard to practice a giving, sacrificial form of married love. That includes learning to forgive each other for our faults and foibles. We have a Christ-centered relationship that has thrived in spite of all our struggles during six decades together. And if you are wondering, it's an ongoing process.

3) We have worked on and remodeled our relationship during each stage of our marriage. There are times when we have grown distant from each other, but we have found ways to bring ourselves back together. We are living proof that it's not the number of times you fall that counts, it's the number of times you get up. After many renovations, our union remains strong and continues to fit us just fine.

2) What are we going to do?

Jim wants to fish.
Lara prefers to be with the grandkids.
In most cases, both husband and wife can enjoy their dream retirement

scenario—at least in part—if they can work together to realize each other's goals. They certainly have more time to pursue their dreams in retirement than they did during their go-go years of kids and work.

In other cases, couples struggle to define what it is they want to do after work is no longer dominating their lives. The questions are many:

- Are we going to design a new and different lifestyle for ourselves, or are we basically going to continue doing what we have been doing for years, even though there is now no work/career in the picture?
- Are we going to do everything together, or will retirement also give us opportunities to more fully develop our individual interests and passions?
- Do we need to do some kind of work, either to help with cash flow or keep us engaged in the world? Or have we had it with our career, and now want to leave that in the rearview mirror as quickly as possible.
- Is there something else we want to do to live out our faith in God, love our neighbors, serve our community, and impact our world? Do we want to volunteer for a charitable organization? Do we want to go on a month-long mission trip to Timbuktu?
- Is there something new God is calling us to do in this season of our lives?

One man retired with the dream of finally finishing work on the antique car that had been occupying part of the garage for the last 15 years. After retirement, he got to work. Within two months the project was done.

"What am I going to do now?" he asked me. "I've got this great classic car, but where am I going to go?"

One woman retired with the dream of finally organizing all the family photos that had been overflowing boxes and bins for years. After retirement, she organized and documented every photo. The whole process took six weeks. Afterwards, she flailed around looking for something else to keep her occupied.

What are you going to do during the 10, 20, or 30 years you will spend in retirement? The best time to start figuring that out is *before* you retire.

God has a plan for each of us. Our job is to discover that plan, follow it, and experiencer the joy, meaning and purpose that comes from pursuing our calling.

3) Where are we going to do it?

Jim and Lara disagree over whether Idaho or Mississippi offers the best retirement options. Welcome to one of the biggest questions you will face in retirement: ***Do we keep our current house, or sell it and move somewhere else?***

Many couples downsize in retirement by selling the big house they lived in when there were kids underfoot, and moving to an apartment or condo that's smaller, less expensive, and easier to clean and manage.

Sounds simple, but many questions must be answered:

- How much of our old stuff do we need and want to keep?
- What kind of new living space do we want?
- Do we want to move where we can be closer to kids and grandkids?
- Or do we want to move into a retirement community in Florida or Sun City, Arizona?
- Or do we want to live in an area near doctors' offices?
- Or do we want to get out of Dodge, leave it all behind, and get off the grid?

Many couples answer these questions based on what they can afford. Many decide the only way they can enjoy the kind of lifestyle they want with the limited retirement savings they have accrued is by moving to expatriate communities in Mexico, Central or Latin America, or southeast Asia. Perhaps you are among the many people who have played the "what if" game? What if we moved to Guatemala? Or Indonesia? Or Laos? Remember too, there are stages in retirement. Each decision must be open to review as you transition to the next stage.

Do we want to move where we can be closer to kids and grandkids? Or do we want to move into a retirement community in Florida or Sun City, Arizona?

Others completely ditch the idea of having a permanent residence or address, and instead sell the house, buy a motorhome or recreational vehicle, and spend their next life stages migrating from place to place. Some choose a simple travel trailer that attaches to a truck or car and sells for $5,000 to $70,000. Others go for a Class A motorhome that's a true home on wheels built on top of a truck or bus chassis. These massive gas hogs can cost $100,000 to well over $1 million. And the older one gets, the more challenging it becomes to empty one tank (septic tank) and fill the other (the 60-gallon gas tank).

There are many ways to answer the "Where?" questions of retirement, and the best time to start tackling them is before you retire. But remember, the "where" questions can't be separated from the "what," "how," and "why" questions of retirement.

4) Who are we going to do it with?

Whether you are single or married, you need other people in your life. But retirement often plays havoc with people's social rituals and networks.

After years and years when coworkers and professional associates were the people you typically associated and socialized with, who are you going to hang out with once work is over? As some people discover too late in the process, it takes time to build and deepen relationships.

If couples move, they will need to find social networks in their new location. But even if they stay put, past networks of friends and associates may change over time.

Everyone needs to answer questions about how the following people and groups will fit into their lives in retirement:

- Family. Do you want to spend more time with them, or less? Do you want to be closer to them, or farther away?
- Parents. If your parents are still alive, caring for them in their later years may complicate your efforts to enjoy your own later years.
- Siblings. Do you have brothers and sisters? What is your relationship with them? And what do you want that relationship to look like in the years ahead?

- Kids. Are they near or far from you? Are you engaged with them or have relationships become estranged? And do they even want to spend more time with you?
- Grandkids. How many are there, and in how many different regions of the country? How much time do you want to spend with them? How will you organize and finance grandparent time?
- Other social networks. Some networks may survive your departure from work, but others may fall apart once you are no longer required report to an office. Can you be more involved in your existing networks? Or are there new networks you want to join or create?
- Community. Which people are your people? Where can you find members of your tribe? Who are the people you want to be with and stay in close communication?
- Church. Many people experience the joy of the Lord in the context of Christian community. If you stay in place, will you get more involved in your church? Will you get involved in a new church if you move? Is retirement your chance to get more involved in the life of a congregation, serving it with your talents, your additional time, and any other resources you may have?
- Other spiritual networks. Spiritual growth takes place outside of churches on Sunday mornings. Are their prayer groups, men's and women's groups, or other interest-based groups you can be a part of to help grow your own spiritual life while also supporting others?

The absence of such social networks can spell trouble for some people. A friend recently to told me they had moved her 93 year old mother from her home in Pennsylvania to Colorado Springs so they could watch over her. She is in a care facility, now cut off from the social networks she had left. She is ill-equipped to make new friends.

"I was afraid that one day I would get a call saying she had fallen and broken her hip, or something worse," she told me.

When your social world shrinks, finding ways to expand it again is hard work. Without preparation, it is almost impossible.

It's a big world, and there are many opportunities for you to connect with people. Who are you going to connect with, and how? As we grow older, our world shrinks. Friends die, move away or become incapacitated. Expanding our community, not shrinking it, is a priority for aging.

5) How are we going to finance it?

When you worked, managing your income was as simple as having your employer automatically deposit your checks into your bank or credit union account. But as with so many other issues, life in retirement can be much more complicated than life was before.

Surveys show that 75% of people in retirement age are anxious about money. Some are anxious about not having enough. Others are driven crazy by trying to manage and balance multiple streams of income instead of just a paycheck.

These are the five most significant income streams in retirement:

- Pension/401k/403b/403(b)(9);
- IRA;
- Inheritance/other savings/real estate;
- Social Security;
- Part time work or consulting.

Some people enjoy income from all of these streams. Others have just one or two of these streams and supplement their cash flow with savings. Each one needs to be managed.

No matter how many streams of income you have, or how big your savings are, your financial resources are finite, which means you need to answer some tough questions:

- Do you have enough to make it last through two or three decades of retirement?
- What about Social Security. When will one or both of you start taking Social Security income?
- How much are you going to take out of your retirement accounts?
- How will you pay for housing, meals, living expenses, and medical care?

These are important but complicated questions, and they have been known to trip up even some couples who have successfully navigated previous money discussions.

According to the brilliant book, <u>The 5 Money Personalities: Speaking the Same Love and Money Language</u>, written by the two brilliant authors, Bethany and Scott Palmer (that's my daughter and her husband), men and women exhibit a variety of approaches. There are spenders and savers. There are risk takers and security seekers.

Couples are more successful in navigating the financial side of retirement if they learn to understand and appreciate each other's unique money personalities. And the sooner you can understand each others' money personalities, the sooner you can learn to work together for your mutual benefit and happiness. It is important to be on the same page, or at least understand the other's page.

6) What is most important to me in retirement?

Item #1 on Larry's bucket list is the Sun. That's because Larry is waiting to retire so he can become a full-fledged Umbraphile.

According to *Fortune* magazine, there are some 50,000 Umbraphiles: people who study the skies so they can schedule travel to locations where they can observe solar eclipses. They were out in mass on August 21, 2017, the most recent total solar eclipse.

Travel-related experiences rank high on many bucket lists. Where do you dream of going?

Other retirees-in-waiting have different dreams they want to fulfill.

Buying a big motorhome and driving from city to city to see spring training for Major League Baseball teams.

Finally reaching a hard-to-reach destination, such as Machu Picchu, Easter Island, or Mount Everest.

Buying ever more expensive toys: Home entertainment system, temperature-controlled wine cellar, or pricey sports car.

When people retire, there are often years' worth of unfulfilled dreams and repressed desires they hope they will now finally get to act on. But the bucket list items described above would wipe out most retirees' savings. Again, these priorities too will require re-examination as you transition from one retirement stage to another. These issues look different at 90 than they do at 70, 60 or 50.

When people retire, there are often years' worth of unfulfilled dreams and repressed desires they hope they will now finally get to act on.

Some people would rather spend more time with friends and family than scale distant mountains. Others see retirement as a fresh opportunity to give more attention to intellectual, artistic, and creative pursuits. Others want to devote more time to beloved hobbies. Still others see their retirement years as a chance to focus more on health, exercise and diet?

In my case, the retirement years have provided a chance for me to pursue my passion for helping people rethink retirement. I'm using the time I have to write this book and do other activities to empower fellow revolutionaries who will help older believers continue using their gifts and talents for God's glory during their retirement years, rather than "retiring" these talents to play shuffleboard or bridge. This work can be demanding, but it is rewarding, and it brings me joy.

Here is a good definition worth embracing: A vision is a picture of God's preferred future fueling your passion to achieve it.

It's been a long life, and there are a lot of dreams you still want to fulfill. But you may not be able to fulfill them all with the finite finances and lifespan you have left.

Still, you could have decades more to live, and there's a lot you can do if you make it happen. So, what is it that's really important to you? Retirement has given you *freedom from* many things. What is retirement giving you the *freedom to do*, and how will you do it? If God has given you a vision, He will provide the capacity and tools to fulfill the call.

A Tricky Transition

I hope your head is not spinning with all these questions. But if your head is spinning, maybe you will concur with what I said earlier: Life in retirement can be a whole lot more complicated than life before retirement.

Some manage the work to retirement transition easily and quickly find a new way to live unencumbered by the duties and burdens of the past. Most do not!

Others find the transition too tricky to navigate, and wind up experiencing financial, social, or spiritual challenges that make the old days of working 9-to-5 seem like a relative picnic.

You can't control everything. The rise or fall of the stock market is beyond your control. But there is much you can control as long as you don't ignore the six essential questions of retirement:

1. How are we going to relate to each other?
2. What are we going to do?
3. Where are we going to do it?
4. Who are we going to do it with?
5. How are we going to finance it?
6. What is most important in retirement?

Think and pray about these questions. Talk to your partner about them. Pray with your partner for God's guidance in finding the best way forward. The better your answers, the better your future in the years to come.

Questions for reflection:

1. Can you, or should you, ignore the issues about or the reality of retirement?
2. What three questions about retirement are the relevant, interesting, or pressing to you?
   a. ?
   b. ?
   c. ?
3. Which of those had you not considered before?
4. What were the big take-aways for you from this chapter?

CHAPTER 8

THE LONGEVITY PREMIUM: SIX GREAT BENEFITS OF AGING THAT SENIORS SAVOR

After playing Hawkeye Pierce on the popular TV show *M*A*S*H* for more than a decade, the Emmy Award winner Alan Alda continued performing on TV and in movies. Then, in the summer of 2018, he made an announcement. He had been diagnosed with Parkinson's disease three years earlier.

Alda made his announcement on a morning TV show, anticipating that fans might write him off or that entertainment journalists might write "a story about this from a sad point of view," he said. "But that's not where I am," said Alda, who declared he was A-OK and continuing on with his life and creative work.

"The reason I want to talk about it in public is that I was diagnosed three and a half years ago, and I've had a full life since," he said on the broadcast.

Alda said his announcement was also intended to send a message to older people fearful of Parkinson's or other debilitating diseases.

"You still have things you can do," said the 82-year-old Alda. To prove his point, he announced he would also be starting a new podcast entitled, *Clear + Vivid with Alan Alda.*

Alda's response to his diagnosis was much more upbeat than that of another famous actor who received the same bad diagnosis four years earlier.

The comedy actor Robin Williams was diagnosed with Parkinson's in May 2014. A few months later, at the age of 63, he took his own life. (The diagnosis turned out to be inaccurate. Williams actually suffered from Lewy body disease, a debilitating form of dementia.)

Friends and family members say Williams was troubled by his declining ability to keep up the rapid-fire banter that used to fuel his stand-up comedy appearances.

Two famous actors.

Two contrasting approaches to old age and its ailments.

Alda and Williams represent two contrasting views many hold about aging.

Two Contrasting Views of Aging

As I talk to people about their ideas of life in retirement, I hear two basic views of the path they will walk in the years to come.

One view is pessimistic. Aging and growing older constitutes a long, dehumanizing, and depressing downhill slog through various ailments of body and mind. And then you die.

The other view—which happens to be my view—is more hopeful. Sure, aging brings challenges, and life ultimately ends in death. But meanwhile, the last 30 years of your life can truly be the best, most productive, and most fulfilling years of your entire life.

Some see the retirement years as a long, dehumanizing, and depressing downhill slog through various ailments of body and mind, ending in death. But I believe your last 30 years can truly be the best, most productive, and most fulfilling years of your entire life.

This view acknowledges that while we *can't choose* how rapidly our bodies and minds will deteriorate, or when we will die, we *can choose* how we respond to these declines and what we will do with our lives in the meantime.

When I'm speaking to a group and making the case that the last 30 years of life can be the best, I almost always hear someone accuse me of ignoring the downsides of aging. But I'm not ignoring anything. I would like to ignore the pains my aging joints create, but I can't. Ditto with my maturing mind, which doesn't multitask quite as well as it once did.

Aging takes a toll on our bodies and minds but aging also brings good gifts that can help our closing decades finish strong!

Our ambiguous feelings about the good and bad that come with aging has been with us for ages, says historian Georges Minois in his book, *History of Old Age: From Antiquity to the Renaissance:* "The problem of the ambiguity of old age has been with us since the stage of primitive society; it was both the source of wisdom and of infirmity, experience and decrepitude, of prestige and suffering."

In this chapter we will explore the six major benefits of something I call the Longevity Premium. Like a loving marriage or good bottle of wine, some things only get better with age. That includes you and me.

Let's see how the Longevity Premium can impact your life by focusing on the six benefits of aging that compensate for some of the physical and mental challenges that do come with age.

Longevity Premium #1: Wisdom

Two people look at the same hill, trying to evaluate the steepness of its slope. One person is 22 years old, while the other is 64.

Scientists wanted to know: Which person was more accurate in assessing the steepness of the slope, the younger person or the older person?

According to researchers at Swarthmore College, the older people with greater life experience are more accurate in sizing up the hill. As the 2016 headline in the online publication sciencedaily.com put it: "New study confirms adage that with age comes wisdom."

This contemporary research confirms ancient biblical teaching on wisdom, which is available to people of all ages, but is often more evident among those of us who have more than a few decades under our belts.

The Old Testament book of Proverbs contains many of the Bible's 200+ references to wisdom, and these passages describe the many benefits of wisdom:

- For wisdom will enter your heart, and knowledge will be pleasant to your soul (Proverbs 2:10);
- Wisdom will save you from the ways of wicked men, from men whose words are perverse (2:12);
- Wisdom will save you also from the adulterous woman, from the wayward woman with her seductive words (2:16);
- Do not forsake wisdom, and she will protect you; love her, and she will watch over you (4:6);
- Wisdom is more precious than rubies, and nothing you desire can compare with her (8:11);
- For through wisdom your days will be many, and years will be added to your life (9:11);
- Where there is strife, there is pride, but wisdom is found in those who take advice (13:10);
- How much better to get wisdom than gold, to get insight rather than silver! (16:16);
- The one who gets wisdom loves life; the one who cherishes understanding will soon prosper (19:8);
- A person's wisdom yields patience; it is to one's glory to overlook an offense (19:11);
- A man who loves wisdom brings joy to his father, but a companion of prostitutes squanders his wealth (29:3);
- Where there is no revelation, people cast off restraint; but blessed is the one who heeds wisdom's instruction (29:18).

If insanity can be described as "doing the same thing over and over again, but expecting different results," wisdom can be described as "learning to not do the same thing over and over again but devising better solutions to bring about better results."

If insanity can be described as "doing the same thing over and over again, but expecting different results," wisdom can be described as "learning to not do the same thing over and over again but devising better solutions to bring about better results."

One example from my own life shows how wisdom has a way of

sneaking up on us as we age. I was 16 years old when I started smoking cigarettes, convinced smoking was cool, or manly, or exciting. Sixteen years later I was still smoking and had absolutely no intention of stopping, even though I had heard the health warnings and seen the disturbing commercials showing the grisly impact tobacco has on the human body.

Then our daughter Bethany went to middle school, where well-meaning teachers filled her innocent mind with all sorts of health information, including the dangers of smoking. Soon, Bethany began pleading with me to finally stop this disgusting and destructive habit.

That didn't get her very far. My defenses remained firm. So, Bethany talked to Judy to get her advice about how to motivate me to change.

"Make him a deal he can't refuse," Judy wisely advised her. Soon after, Bethany came at me with an ingenious approach:

"Dad," she said, "I will be going into high school next year, and you probably don't want me to smoke, drink, or do drugs. Is that right?"

"That's right."

"Well, then, if I promise not to smoke, drink, or do drugs, plus I promise to do my absolute best to make it to the national swim team, will you stop your smoking?"

As I paused to consider her offer, she added a clincher.

"And if you do stop, but fail and have another cigarette, you will need to buy me a car."

I was positively trapped by Judy's wisdom and Bethany's application.

Bethany appealed to me on a Tuesday. The next Friday morning I quit cold turkey, handing a half-smoked package of cigarettes to Judy. That was 45 years ago. I haven't had one cigarette since.

Bethany's compelling offer was certainly part of my decision to quit smoking, but I also chalk part of my decision up to wisdom. Bethany made her offer when I was 32 years old. By that time, I was no longer quite as attached to the superficial trappings of coolness as I was when I started smoking at age 16.

Of course, not every older person is wise, but as a general rule, wisdom comes with age, and a lifetime of experience can pay big dividends.

As we grow older and wiser, we bring more experience to the table each time we face a new challenge. And the lessons we've learned from previous bad choices help us make better choices in the future.

My grandfather once asked me why experience is the best teacher? Following my shrug, he declared, "Because it is the most expensive." We remember our costly mistakes. Wisdom is the result. Experience is the best teacher, passing on to us valuable and often difficult lessons. In my remaining years, I want to experience more of this Longevity Premium by understanding and applying the lessons I've learned, as well as lessons taught to me by others.

Longevity Premium #2: Spiritual Growth

Just as wisdom seems to grow with age, we can experience spiritual growth and renewal during our retirement years. As previous obligations, duties and desires fall by the wayside, we suddenly have more time to invest in prayer, reflection, Bible study, and fellowship with a community of believers.

According to one of many recent studies on spirituality and aging, there is "overwhelming evidence of positive health outcomes linked to spirituality and religious participation." In addition, older people place a higher priority on spirituality as other parts of life become more vulnerable to the potential ravages of aging. "Understanding individual spiritual perspectives becomes increasingly important, given the issues of loss, physical illness and mortality that are confronted in old age."

My faith has been important to me for years, but as I age, I can see that spiritual disciplines and practices that were once difficult or unimportant to me are not only more important but also easier for me to practice and enjoy. It's like the hymn says:

Just a closer walk with Thee
Grant it, Jesus, is my plea
Daily walking close to Thee
Let it be, dear Lord, let it be

As I have matured, I am experiencing the closer walk with God this hymn describes. I rest in His plan, His care, and His direction for my life—at least until I try to take control back and run everything myself.

The late Eugene Peterson worked as a Christian pastor, a bestselling author, and translator of the contemporary Bible, *The Message*. He once described discipleship as "a long obedience in the same direction." As

Bruce Bruinsma

Peterson explained, that kind of commitment to God is rare in our age of sensation and emotion:

"There is a great market for religious experience in our world; there is little enthusiasm for the patient acquisition of virtue, little inclination to sign up for a long apprenticeship in what earlier generations of Christians called holiness."

When I was younger, so many things competed for my attention, often drowning out God's still, small voice. But as I've grown older, my heart seems more attuned to God, more sensitive to His work in my life, and more committed to following His will for me, no matter what that is.

Like my long and loving relationship with Judy, my long and loving relationship with God grows deeper and stronger every day. When one is faithful for a lifetime, one can experience this kind of continuous and growing relationship with God. I look forward each day to studying God's word, praying to Him as I share my praises and petitions, and hearing what he has to say to me. When I listen, He speaks!

Like my long and loving relationship with Judy, my long and loving relationship with God grows deeper and stronger every day.

God has loved me all my life, and over time that love has left its mark, transforming me into the person whose life increasingly exhibits the fruits of the spirit. Today I am living with more love, joy, peace, patience, kindness, and gentleness, and self-control than I ever experienced before. And the best is yet to come! These fruits are promised to every Christian who is walking with God. They are promised to you.

Longevity Premium #3: Meaning and Purpose

People choose many different ways to live out their retirement years. As we saw in Chapters 3 and 4, many devote their remaining years to a life of leisure or the pursuit of "nothing."

I understand why many people make these choices. After decades of work and obligations, there's a pent-up demand to spend time kicking back. There's a huge hunger for freedom from all the things that made life seem so complex.

But "nothing" isn't a strong enough foundation to support a meaningful life. I can see this when I talk to some who have opted for a lifestyle of relaxation and consumption. There's a narrowness—or a shallowness—to their lives, an absence of things that matter or make a difference. From what I see, a life based on nothing or leisure is a recipe for depression.

During their working years, people talk of trying to establish a healthy work-life balance. In retirement, there's a different kind balance we need to find. I call it the meaning-pleasure balance.

I believe many Sun City residents would be happier and more joyful if they balanced the meaningful with the pleasurable. Playing golf every day can become boring and routine after five, ten or twenty years. While golf can be a fun and stimulating as a "spice of life," it's not meaty enough to be the main course.

When I speak about decades of retirement dedicated to nothing or leisure, people often ask me, "Well, what *should* we be spending our lives doing?" They get a little defensive.

I'm so glad they ask, and my answer invariably cites the Westminster Catechism, which Presbyterian Sunday school students have learned for centuries. (It's also known as the Heidelberg Catechism, or Reformed Catechism.) Lessons are presented in a series of questions and answers, and the first question is an important one.

Question: **What is the chief end of man?**
Answer: Man's chief end is to glorify God, and to enjoy him forever.

(By the way, glorifying and enjoying God is *women's* chief end, too. They didn't use much gender-neutral language back in the day.) Chief end is another way to say "priority."

There's plenty of time in a day to glorify and enjoy God in addition to playing a nice game of golf. But I prefer to put first things first. God outranks golf—or pretty much anything else—in my book.

When I talk to people who are still working but getting ready for retirement, there are things they crave because their work, family duties and other responsibilities prevented them from enjoying them. Sometimes this craving is overpowering. But these desires aren't the basis for a meaningful 24/7 existence. These fun activities don't give life a basis for *meaning and purpose.*

I encourage people who are preparing for retirement to change their thinking.

Retirement is not a transition from work to leisure.

Retirement is a transition from one kind of work to another: From work someone else is paying me to do, to work that uses my gifts and talents and serves God's kingdom purposes.

What kind of work? That's between you and God to figure out. I recommend *realistic* activity. This means it's something you are prepared and equipped to do:

- It's something you are physically and mentally prepared to do or capable of doing.
- It's something that helps you glorify and enjoy God more every day.
- It's something that helps you love your neighbor.

You have a freedom in retirement you may never have experienced since you were a child. Return to that childhood innocence for a moment to take a fresh look at your life. Think of all you can be, and all you can do, to reflect Jesus with all your being and all your doing.

Living with meaning is much better than the fruitless, meaningless and self-absorbed pursuit of pleasure, no matter what age you are. The Longevity Premium helps us see which work is right for us at this stage of our life.

When you learn to combine the Longevity Premium of spiritual growth with the Longevity Premium of meaning and purpose, you are ready for a retirement revolution. Meaning and purpose grow and deepen as you connect with God's plan in each stage of your life. Because I remain connected to God, I remain committed to impacting the kingdom in new ways, with growing wisdom and more fruits of His spirit.

Longevity Premium #4: Greater Emotional Maturity

Perhaps you have heard of something called "emotional intelligence." Social scientists use the term to describe people who understand and are aware of their own emotions, conscious of and sensitive to the emotions of others around them, and able to use this rich trove of information to navigate all manner of complex social and relational situations.

I am the poster child for this longevity benefit. Early on in my career, it was embarrassingly easy for other people to push my buttons and make me react with anger or other emotions that were inappropriate or even hurtful. Even the silliest or the least substantial things could set me off and make me respond in ways that would surprise both myself and those around me.

Thank God that my Emotional Intelligence Quotient has been rising over the years. Comments or actions that previously would have set me off now intrigue me. Instead of reacting to what someone says or does, I try to understand it, learn and grow from it.

What makes the difference between the way I react now and the way I reacted when I was younger and had a lower EIQ? Part of it is learning from my mistakes. Part of it is greater patience and grace with others. Much of it comes from getting to know myself better, understanding of various emotions that can be stirred up within me, and learning how to channel my feelings into positive outcomes for myself and the people I live and work with. And then, there is that close walk with God.

Paul articulates something of this process in his famous "love" chapter: "When I was a child, I talked like a child, I thought like a child, I reasoned like a child. When I became a man, I put the ways of childhood behind me" (1 Corinthians 13: 11.)

People are complicated. Every human relationship we have is going to generate its share of challenges, tests, and potential offenses. I'm grateful that I'm learning more every day about how to speak into and deal with difficult interpersonal relationships in loving, redemptive and positive ways.

For the longest time I thought I could navigate life with head knowledge and intellectual intelligence. No more. Now I have a more balanced approach to dealing with the challenges that come through being connected to family, friends, and fellow believers. My life has been much richer and more pleasurable as I've learned to gradually raise my EIQ.

Longevity Premium #5: Contentment

A beautiful sunrise in the morning.

A cup of coffee and conversation with a friend.

A nice dinner with loved ones.

A setting sun accompanied by a chorus of birds.

These are some of the pleasures I get to experience many days of my life, and over time I've learned to appreciate and savor them more deeply every day.

Welcome to contentment, the Longevity Benefit that some have called "the incredible lightness of being older."

When I was younger, I was less content because I was constantly striving and working toward the next big thing. I'm still working—in some ways harder than ever before—but the desperation has disappeared. I'm doing what I do today out of a sense of gratefulness, service, and not striving. I'm receiving what God shares with me and sharing it with others.

Women can experience the Longevity Premium of contentment, too, as writer Margaret Renkl showed in her essay for *The New York Times*, "The Surprising Gift of Menopause." She opens with regrets: "There are things I miss about being fertile. A waistline. Hair thick enough to hide my pink scalp and skin fitted enough to prove I have bones."

But after acknowledging many ravages of aging, she focuses on the blessings. "I feel more keenly than ever the bounty of this beautiful, temporary life," she writes. Here she explains some of this surprising gift:

"The pyrotechnics of youth may be gone, but I have learned that there's no aphrodisiac like long love, like the feeling of knowing and being known, of belonging to a beloved's body as fully as you belong to your own.

"And it's easier now to shrug off failure. It's easier to shrug off most other things, too: missed opportunities, the unwarranted anger of others, fear of looking like a fool. A person who is not afraid of looking like a fool gets to do a lot more dancing."

Like Renkl, I have my share of regret, and I sometimes grieve the losses I experience in aging. But I find the gnawing anxieties that tormented me during my younger years have given way to a greater sense of overall contentment and gratitude for everything I have experienced thus far.

And I'm looking forward to tomorrow's sunrise.

Longevity Premium #6: Increased Capacity for Service and Leadership

I've enjoyed all five of the Longevity Premiums described above, but I can clearly say that number six is my number one favorite. Put simply: there's more bang for the buck. I'm working better, more productively, more completely, and with greater intentionality than I ever have before.

Actually, the five preceding longevity benefits build upon each other to bring the increased capacity older people can experience in their lives:

- The wisdom to choose wisely what we will do;
- The long-term intimacy with God that sensitizes us to his voice and his will for our lives;
- The energy that seems to flow from deep within whenever we are engaged in activities that have meaning and purpose;
- The enhanced emotional intelligence that helps us navigate complex people and situations for the good of all;
- The blessing of contentment, which leads to work that is focused and intentional rather than driven and striving.

While many people think of retirement as the time in life when they can finally *stop doing* all manner of things, I see retirement as the time in life when people can finally *start doing* more of the tasks that fit their calling and equipping.

Try it, and you will see for yourself. You can accomplish more now than you ever could before.

A Second Chance

I've seen the pessimistic sentiment about aging expressed on bumper stickers and in cartoons: "Getting old is a bummer!" My mother often reflected, "Getting old is not for sissies!"

Yes, aging has its much-discussed disadvantages, but aging also offers little-explored advantages that can make this season of life the most exciting, successful, and fulfilling season of all.

Instead of seeing your post-work years as a slow, downward slog, embrace them as the glorious opportunity they are. The ten, twenty or thirty years of life you may have in retirement can be your second chance to do some of the things you have been wanting to do for decades, and thanks to the various Longevity Premiums, you can do them better, or more effectively, than you could have when you were younger and less wise.

Questions for Reflection

There were 6 longevity premiums listed in the chapter: Review them now, perhaps write them down

1) What's your view? Do you see the coming years of retirement as a long, downward slog? Or do you view the future as a golden opportunity to achieve things you couldn't before? Or are you somewhere in between?

2) Take another look at the six Longevity Premiums in this chapter. Have you experienced any of these benefits yourself? How?

3) How do you think you could use your retirement years to deepen your spiritual life?

4) Do you ever feel God is calling you to assignments that you were not able to fulfill during your working life?

CHAPTER 9

PREPARING FOR THE THREE STAGES OF RETIREMENT

Martin Hurkens always dreamed of being an opera singer, but life intervened. Too poor to stay in music school long enough to earn a degree, he worked as a baker for three decades to support his family. He still sang whenever he could, but his primary audience was friends and loved ones.

Then life intervened again. Martin lost his baker job. He remained unemployed as the months turned into years. That's when his daughter had an idea.

"In 2010, my youngest daughter signed me up for the RTL program 'Holland's Got Talent' behind my back," said the Netherlands native. "After some hesitation, I decided to participate in this great program."

He not only participated, but this unknown, unemployed baker stole the show and won the competition. Since then, he's performed in New York City, China, Taiwan, Japan, Italy, France, Turkey and Germany. He also performs regularly with symphony orchestras in the Netherlands. And more than 16 million people have seen a YouTube clip featuring Martin singing a lovely version of Josh Groban's "You Lift Me Up" in the center square of the city of Maastricht (https://bit.ly/2zdgevZ).

"Being an unemployed baker, a new world was suddenly opening up for me!" he said. "Singing has always been my hobby and passion and now there was an opportunity to turn my hobby into my profession, so I seized it with both hands. That's why I say, you may always dream, and sometimes they will even come true."

Pursuing Our Dreams

I love Martin's voice, but more than that, I love his approach toward life. After decades of devotion to his job, Martin had a chance to live out one his treasured dreams. Thanks to his unplanned unemployment—along with a little prodding from his daughter—he jumped at the chance.

For me, Martin is a powerful symbol of potentiality. He represents opportunities each one of us has to use our retirement years to finally pursue dreams that we've been preparing for all our lives.

Many people look forward to retirement as a time of leisure, relaxation, or "doing nothing." That's completely understandable. But I believe many of these folks are missing a glorious opportunity to finally do something they've never been able to do before: Live out some of their dreams that were deferred or delayed for years and years. Different people have different dream lists or "Bucket Lists:"

- Some dream of starting new careers.
- Some dream of using their skills and expertise to serve others.
- Some dream of having the time they need to develop deeper relationships with family members or friends.
- Some dream of devoting more time to reading and study, or beloved hobbies.
- Some dream of finally obeying a calling that God placed on their lives.

Martin Hurkens dreamed of singing, and when opportunity knocked, he pursued that dream with all his might. He's a retirement role model who reminds us that there's plenty of time for us to pursue our dreams in retirement.

Preparing for Retirement's Three Different Stages

It's been this way for centuries: Life consists of a decades-long working phase, which is followed by a brief retirement phase of perhaps a few years, which is rapidly followed by death.

People who retire today may spend half (or more) of their lives in retirement.

It's not that way anymore. Thanks to the Longevity Revolution we explored in Chapter 5, many of us will actually spend two or three decades in retirement.

In other words, the time we spend *in retirement* may equal half or more of the time we spent living *before retirement*. That's why it's so important for you to plan for your retirement years. There is so much time to miss the opportunities. So many opportunities that can go unrealized. In business we call it "lost opportunity."

And I have news for you: Not all retirement years are created equal. Your first year of retirement will offer different challenges and opportunities than your last year of retirement. Your life at age 70 will be different from your life at age 95.

Retirement is not one long homogenous season of life, but rather thousands of days, each with its own issues and challenges, its own options and choices, and its own opportunities to hear God's will and serve His Kingdom anew.

That's why we need to prepare for the ***Three Stages of Retirement***. If you like, you can also think of these stages as different seasons or phases you will go through during the decades you spend in retirement.

Over the years, as I have watched hundreds of men and women make their way through the journey of retirement, it has become clear that most people actually experience retirement in three stages:

- The ***Active*** stage, when we finally have a chance to accomplish all the wonderful things we couldn't accomplish before.

- The ***Mentoring*** stage, when we can utilize the experiences and insights we have gained to have an impact on our community and our world.
- The ***Sharing*** stage, when we use whatever time we have left to shower blessings on our loved ones and encourage them while also focusing on ending well.

Let's examine these three stages to see where you are and what you can do to make the most of the time and resources you have.

Retirement Stage 1: Active (Age 67 to 76)

Martin Hurkens dreamed of being an opera singer, and even though his dream was delayed, his decades of experience singing and training his voice gave him the preparation he needed when he finally had his chance to enter a competition and sing for the world.

What have you dreamed of doing during retirement? Whatever it is, now is the time to start pursuing it with all your energy, because the first decade of retirement is the most active stage. This is the stage of doing, the stage of starting new dream projects, the stage of finally getting to work on all the things you wanted to do before but never had the time or energy to do.

What have you dreamed of doing during retirement? The Active stage is the time to start pursuing it with all your energy. A time to be passionate about God's call on your life.

Some people say there's no such things as second chances. "You make your bed, now you lie in it," they say. The past predicts the future. But don't tell that to Ronald Reagan, Arnold Schwarzenegger, Al Franken, Fred Thompson, or Jesse Ventura—all of whom had first careers in entertainment before transitioning to second careers in politics.

I describe the Active stage as running from age 67 to 76. I start at 67 because that's the official retirement age as detailed by the Social Security Administration in the U.S., even though some people actually retire in their 50s. I describe the Active stage as lasting ten years, but the precise timing is different for different people, even though the key principles remain.

For Margaret Thatcher, the daughter of a Methodist preacher and local politician, a brief career in chemistry was a prelude to a life in politics. She was 54 when she became the first female Prime Minister in British history. By the time she resigned in 1990 at age 65, the "Iron lady" had become the longest serving Prime Minister in British history.

But Thatcher wasn't through doing things quite yet. She spent the rest of her life serving as a member of the House of Lords and running her own charitable foundation (she was the first former prime minister to start one) before being diagnosed with dementia and dying at the age of 87.

Do you have a few dreams you've always wanted to pursue? The Active stage of retirement offers your best chance to pursue them. If you don't, God has one for you!

Primary Tasks of the Active Stage of Retirement

People approach the first stage of retirement with a mixture of excitement, uncertainty, and even indifference.

They're glad for a chance to do something different from what they've always done.

They're amazed at how quickly the years have flown by.

They're not sure how their remaining time will play out.

They're wiser than they were before. They have a clearer picture of the true meaning and value of life. And they want to spend more time doing things that have meaning, purpose, and value.

We call this stage of retirement the Active stage because most people in this stage have the energy, passion, and physical and mental strength to do what they want to do. They must seize the day, because these physical strengths and abilities typically decrease during the following stages of retirement. Remember, we grow stronger spiritually and emotionally offsetting the physical decline.

I also emphasize activity because many retirees dream of kicking back and doing "nothing." As we have seen, nothing may be fine for a time, but it's not a good foundation for living a full and meaningful life. Plus, at some point, it's not fun.

This first stage of retirement is a gift to you. It's your opportunity to do some of the things you always wanted to do but couldn't do because of all your previous commitments and obligations.

What will you do? People in the Active stage focus on a variety of opportunities, and two of the most rewarding seem to be:

- Work that may not feel like work because it's different from the work you have done for years; It fits your preparation and fuels your passion.
- Personal growth and development that you always wanted to do but never had the time or thought you didn't. We mature in our being which is reflected in our doing.

Work that's different. It may seem counterintuitive that people want to work after a lifetime of work, career, or owning a business. The difference is simple. The new work is a different kind of work from the work they've done all their lives. Its work they *want* to do, not work someone else is *telling them* to do.

> So, what is work? An activity involving mental or physical effort done in order to achieve a purpose or result.

The Active stage of retirement may be your best chance to start this work, or perhaps start the study, training and preparation that may be necessary.

For many people, retirement from the job they were doing offers them an opportunity to do the job they've always wanted to do. What's on your list?

- Starting that new company, perhaps one based on your passions and hobbies, or starting that new dream project you've always wanted to start.
- Doing something not because of the money involved, but because of the fulfillment and impact it brings, such as teaching students in an underachieving school.
- Serving, volunteering, and ministering. Christ calls all his followers to serve him, and many of the men and women I've known say

their main goal in retirement is to devote more time and attention to caring for others, sharing their talents and gifts was people who need them, sharing their faith with others, and serving as Christ's loving ambassadors to a hurting and needy world.

- Leading and serving the public, whether it be Prime Minister of England or school board member in your local community. This is your chance to bring about the change you've always wanted to bring. You become an active agent of change. We understand that the definition of ministry is "changed lives." Yours and others through you.

Personal growth and enrichment. Some people have had enough work, thank you. They want to explore other aspects of life, even though they may have to "work" at it.

- Going deeper in relationships. For many, retirement offers more freedom to invest time and energy in spending quality and fun time with others, where that be friends, loved ones, family members, or grandkids.
- Many also see this stage of retirement as an opportunity to go deeper in their relationship with Christ, spending more time in prayer, study, reflection, or active ministry.
- Others embrace an opportunity to go deeper in reading, research, or writing now that they are freed of previous distractions.
- Fun. Grab your big, long Bucket List and start enjoying some of life's wonderful pleasures that were denied you before. If you want to travel, then it's time to hit the road, Jack. If you want to join a local choir, take up a new hobby, or finish restoring that vintage sports car that's been sitting in your garage for decades, here's your chance to go for it! And, reflecting Jesus to the world whatever you are doing.

You may wonder why I put fun last on the list. It's not because I'm a killjoy, but because I've seen too many people put fun on the top of their list only to find they are having less fun then they thought they would, while also running down their retirement savings. If you've put away money for a classy Danube cruise, then enjoy it. But if you haven't put away that money, you may want to consider less costly ways to travel or have fun.

The Active stage of retirement gives you a chance to enjoy some of the things you couldn't enjoy before. But remember: This first phase is all about doing as much as you can and being as active as you can while you can. There will be more time for passive leisure, entertainment and ministry activities later in the following two stages.

And by the way, if you really like what you've been doing all your life thus far, you can keep doing it, and perhaps do it even better than you have before. That's the approach singer Rod Stewart seems to be taking during this phase of his decades-long career, as I saw for myself when his 2018 summer tour landed in Denver.

Although I'm critical of aspects of Stewart's lifestyle, I've followed his long career for decades, from his work with bands like Faces and Jeff Beck, to his solo career, from "Maggie May" to torch light ballads. And I'm pleased to report he's still "got it" at age 73. I was thrilled by his voice, his energy, and his strong foot, which he demonstrated by kicking 50 soccer balls into the farthest reaches of the arena.

Stewart isn't resting on his laurels or his knighthood but is actively Doing and continuing into the future with all the energy he's got. It's a matter of priority.

Your Homework Assignments for the Active Stage

If you want to make the most of the first stage of retirement, make sure you address these three assignments.

1) Make a plan.

Many people enter retirement with a lifetime of dreams and desires but little more than a hodgepodge of ideas about what they're going to do. I've personally seen that retirement works out a whole lot better if people actually have a plan. And following God's plan is the best way to go.

Do you have a plan for what you will do and how you will do it in retirement or at least in the next stage? If not, get started. Grab a notebook or open a Word document and start writing down everything you can think of. Them go back, prioritizing and organizing everything you've written. Keep doing it. Then do it some more. (Planning is an important topic we'll explore more in chapters 10 and 11.)

2) Expand your social world.

As we grow older, the world seems to shrink as we lose contact with old friends from work, as our children and grandchildren pack up and move away, and as other friends and loved ones die off. You may also experience physical limitations that make it harder for you to go out and enjoy social events.

Your world will continue shrinking around you unless you do something intentional to enlarge it. Seek out opportunities to find new friends, improve your relationships with family members who may have grown distant, and find out what kinds of social media and communication technology people are using and learn how to use it yourself to stay in touch with others. Go to church!

3) Get your affairs in order.

What will you leave behind for your survivors if you go out to the golf course today, get conked on the head by an errant drive, and fall over dead? Don't leave your loved ones hanging you're your homework so they know everything they need to know.

- In many cases, people die without a *will*. In other cases, they have a will but haven't updated it in a long, long while. Please don't let this happen to you. Make this one of your priorities.
- While you're at it, make sure you have signed and notarized all relevant *medical directives* that spell out the kind of medical care you want to or don't want to receive.
- Dialogue with your spouse and children about how you are planning to divide your assets.

- In some cases, people benefit from creating a ***Living Trust*** that allows them to utilize their assets now and transfers them to designated beneficiaries after your death. It also means your heirs can bypass the costs and frustrations of probate court.
- And if you don't want someone to sing a schmaltzy version of "Teardrops Keep Fallin' on My Head" at your funeral, you better start a document about your own ***last rites***, as well.

4) Start Preparing now for the next two stages.

The Active stage of retirement takes up only the first third of the retirement years, and there are two-thirds left to go. Devote part of your time and energy in this crucial first stage to deciding and planning what you hope to achieve in the stages that follow. Transitions are important.

Retirement Stage 2: Mentoring (77 to 86 years)

Jane Goodall went to Africa in 1960 to study chimpanzees. She was 26 years old, and the world never would have heard much about her research if she hadn't changed history.

Within three months of arriving in Africa, she saw the chimps turning twigs into tools and using them to pull termites out of a big termite mound. Previously, we humans thought we were the only creatures who used tools, but Goodall's research radically transformed our understanding of animals.

Her story, which was told in the 2017 National Geographic movie, *Jane,* continues today. Now that Goodall is 84, she's focusing on mentoring others to carry on her life's work and her worldwide influence:

- In 1977 she founded the Jane Goodall Institute, a wildlife and environment conservation organization that works in two dozen countries.
- In 1991 she founded Roots & Shoots, which gathers young people from preschool through college to work for environmental,

conservation and humanitarian causes. The organization now has more than 10,000 groups in 100+ countries.

- A few years later the Jane Goodall Institute's Center for Primate Studies was created at the <u>University of Minnesota</u> to house her archives and make them accessible to other researchers.
- In 2002, she was named a <u>UN Messenger of Peace</u>.
- Today she spends some 300 days a year traveling the world to advocate for chimps, other animals, the environment, and veganism.

While these issues may not be yours, you can bring the same passion to your important issues.

Charles Stanley accepted Christ at age 12 and by the time he was 14 he was already involved in Christian ministry. Two decades later he joined the staff of First Baptist Church of Atlanta. Today he remains the church's senior pastor at age 86.

In the 1970s he founded In Touch ministries, reaching millions of people in 50 languages through his audio and video sermons and teaching. His books have sold more than 3.5 million copies. He also served two terms as president of the <u>Southern Baptist Convention</u>.

Stanley has suffered his setbacks, including a divorce and feud with his son, Andy. But the feud has been settled, and today Stanley celebrates his son's success. Andy is pastor of North Point Community Church in Atlanta, which is one of America's largest congregations and has more than 20 "strategic partner" churches around the world.

Charles Stanley is still doing what he loves. As he says, "Life is worth nothing unless I use it for doing the work assigned me by the Lord Jesus— the work of telling others the Good News about God's mighty kindness and love." Let me say again, while these issues may not be yours, you can bring the same passion to your important issues.

In the Mentoring stage of retirement, people utilize the experiences and insights they have gained throughout their lives to instruct, inspire, mentor, coach, and impact many other lives. Passion follows mission.

Jane Goodall and Charles Stanley are good examples of the Mentoring stage of retirement. Both are utilizing the experiences and insights they have gained throughout their lives to instruct, inspire, mentor, coach, and impact many other lives. In some ways, they still do what they always did, but with a deeper respect for the past and a passion for influencing the future.

During the Mentoring stage, many people teach classes or seminars, or they write blogs, articles, or books, all of it designed to help others understand and address our world and be involved in changing it. Sowing the seed that will sprout for Jesus, is active work available to all of us.

The Mentoring stage is the time when people seek to mentor and encourage others, to be a blessing to others, to educate and inspire others to play their roles in the world.

If you're not as famous as Goodall and Stanley, that doesn't mean you don't have an impact on others. You do, and now's a good time to be more intentional about what that impact is.

During you're your long and rewarding years life, you have developed valuable resources, including your experience, your wisdom, and your relationships and connections. Now is the time to use these resources to reach and educate your loved ones, your community, and possibly your world.

Primary Tasks of the "Mentoring" Stage of Retirement

In his popular "Seashells" sermon, pastor John Piper contrasts the different ways people live out their retirement years.

"Three weeks ago, we got news at our church that Ruby Eliason and Laura Edwards were killed in Cameroon," Piper said, explaining that both women were in their 80s and were still actively serving and ministering to sick people and poor people in one of the world's most remote places.

Piper contrasted these two women with a married couple in Florida:

"Bob and Penny took early retirement from their jobs in the Northeast five years ago when he was 59 and she was 51. Now they live in Punta Gorda, Florida, where they cruise on their 30-foot trawler, play softball, and collect shells."

Piper even joked about how Bob and Penny might fare when they stand before God at the day of judgment to explain how they lived their lives: "Here it is, Lord—my shell collection. And I've got a good swing. And look at my boat."

"That's a tragedy," said Piper, who wrote a book called *Don't Waste Your Life* that sold more than 600,000 copies.

I've got nothing against collecting seashells or playing softball. If you love these pastimes, enjoy them! But please don't let anybody tell you that such activities are all there is to life in retirement. Your later years can actually be much fuller and exciting when you listen to God, stay engaged in the world and in other people's lives as a steward.

What do you have to steward? What life lessons have you learned, and how can you pass them on to others? There are many ways to be a good mentor in this stage of life.

- I know many seniors who have decided to research and write family histories that they can give to children and grandchildren to keep the family legacy fresh and alive.
- Other seniors who teach others at school, at Sunday school, in Cameroon (like Ruby and Laura above), or in other settings.
- I know many who are mentoring others by using the decades of biblical and theological knowledge they have gained to lead Bible studies or home groups where they help believers live out their faith.
- The Mentoring stage is also your best timer for mentoring others and helping them navigate their own lives with some of the hard-earned wisdom you have picked up throughout your life journey.

The key activity of the Mentoring stage is making the best use you can of your time, talents, and many treasures to educate, encourage and inspire others to be and impact their world. We can mentor and we can step up another level to coaching. Coaching helps to direct their lives with meaning and purpose.

Your Homework Assignments for the Mentoring Stage

A steward is someone who carefully and responsibly manages resources that have been entrusted to his or her care. The assignments for stewards are similar to the assignments for doers, but there are a few important tweaks.

1) Seek and share wisdom.

Have you learned anything important over the course of your life that might help someone else? Now's the time to figure out what your life lessons have been and find ways to pass them on to others who need them. You may be surprised to see how much wisdom you have to pass on.

Seek out wisdom wherever you can find it: The Bible, history books, wise friends and associates, and through reflection and journaling about your own life journey and the lessons you have learned.

2) Deepen and expand your community.

Spend more time with your spouse and learn to love more deeply. Devote time and energy to having good times and meaningful experiences with kids and grandkids.

Seek out meaningful fellowship with others. And by all means stay active, physically and socially, with a diverse roster of fun hobbies, physical activities, and social networking. Love your spouse, kin, and other close loved ones. Enjoy the experience of sharing your life and heart with those closest to you.

Expand your neighborhood by meeting new people who may have interests and experiences that are different from yours. Continue to develop your relationship skills so you have greater emotional maturity to deal with whatever people do. Build and deepen relationships so that you can deeply share your life lessons with others while also hearing their hearts.

3) Serve and lead.

You've spent a lifetime building your reputation and credibility through all the things you have done. Now is the time to use these resources to serve others.

Search for opportunities to bless others, whether that be as a lowly servant or a high-powered leader. Focus on work that uses your gifts and makes a significant impact rather than furthering away your time on busywork. Explore opportunities to serve on church elder boards, ministry and business boards, or with think tanks.

Some people become proverbial "shrinking violets" when are old because they don't think anyone else cares about what they say. Resist that pressure by being aggressively old. I don't mean you should be rude and nasty, but merely speak with confidence in who you are, who you are in Christ, and what you've learned on your journey through life.

And as you grow in your public service, remember to continue fostering the interior growth of the fruit of the spirit in your life: love, joy, peace, forbearance, kindness, goodness, faithfulness, gentleness and self-control (Galatians 5:22-23).

4) Smell the roses.

Learn to enjoy life by giving your time to things that fuel your jets and feed your soul. Practice appreciating God's grace and goodness in your life and take time to thank him for all his blessings.

The older I am, the more I recognize the fact that I'm not perfect. I can see my weakness and sin more clearly. But that doesn't mean I need to live with never-ending guilt, or that I need to seek some form of sinless perfection. I am free to live a Christ-centered life and one on mission, all because of God's grace.

5) Downshift.

You're not the spring chicken you once were, so give yourself permission to play tennis doubles instead of singles. Know that it's OK to walk a little slower, to use a cart when playing golf, to check your bags when traveling by airplane, and to reflect a moment before answering questions. Learn to downshift and enjoy life at a slower pace than you knew when everything was go-go-go.

6) Get your affairs in order.

Hopefully you tackled this assignment in the previous stage. If so, take a fresh look, updating your plans after talking with your spouse and family and updating relevant information about you, your life, and your retirement funds. If your will and other late-stage documents are in disarray or nonexistent, take some time to do your work on these so you don't leave loved ones lost or conflicted about your last wishes.

7) Start Preparing now for the next stage.

This, too, is a repeat assignment, but now you only have one stage before you, and planning it out well will pay off for you down the road. What do you hope to achieve in the next and final stage of retirement?

Have patience as you look forward to the next stage of your retirement journey. Not everything is a raging fire that you must extinguish this second. Act with wisdom and perseverance. You've already run the course. Now it's time to stay the course.

Retirement Stage 3: Sharing (87 to Eternity)

You have lived a long life. You've spent many decades acquiring wisdom, experience, and assets. Now's your opportunity to give it all away.

There was a bumper sticker a few years back that said, "He who dies with the most toys wins."

There was another bumper sticker that read: "We're busy spending our children's inheritance."

Both may be cute, but neither provides a good motto for our last stage of retirement. I would prefer a bumper sticker that read more like this: "Sharing it all with others while I can!"

There are people all around us living out the Sharing stage of retirement, but we don't see it because we don't know what to look for. Let me introduce you to two people who are spending their final years giving it all away. You know one because he is a global celebrity, but the other one is known only to a few because her work is quieter.

In the Sharing stage of retirement, men and women seek to give their wisdom and wealth to others.

1) The ex-President

People disagree about Jimmy Carter's effectiveness as president, but most agree that Carter has been a great ex-president, thanks to his work as a global ambassador, author, Sunday school teacher, and volunteer laborer for Habitat for Humanity.

Carter's 37 years of post-presidential work makes him a great role model for the Sharing stage of retirement. At the age of 94, Carter is still loving God, still serving his neighbors, and still giving what he has to others. And I believe he may have greater influence in our world today than he had while he was in office.

The Washington Post published a 2018 profile of Carter that was headlined: "The Un-celebrity President: Jimmy Carter shuns riches, lives modestly in his Georgia hometown."

Crowds still line up on Sunday mornings—just like they have for decades—to hear Carter teach Sunday school at Maranatha Baptist Church in his hometown of Plains, Georgia, a town of about 700 people that's south of Atlanta. On one recent Sunday, visitors came from 20 states and four foreign countries to hear Carter's meandering lesson.

I haven't been able to attend one of the 39th president's Sunday school classes, but I read his 32nd book, *Faith*. In it, Carter explains: "To me, 'faith' is not just a noun but also a verb."

He hasn't "cashed in" on his time as president, according to the *Post* profile: "Carter is the only president in the modern era to return full-time to the house he lived in before he entered politics — a two-bedroom rancher assessed at $167,000, less than the value of the armored Secret Service vehicles parked outside."

His simple lifestyle is good for our tax bills. Guarding him costs about half of what the U. S. government spends on other ex-presidents.

Carter has experienced his share of health problems, including melanoma that spread to his liver and his brain. (As he told one of his Sunday school classes, his cancer is now in remission.) By this time in his life, he could take it easy and let the world take care of itself. Instead, he continues sharing to help others who are less fortunate:

Carter has used his post-presidency to support human rights, global health programs and fair elections worldwide through his Carter Center, based in Atlanta. He has helped renovate 4,300 homes in 14 countries for Habitat for Humanity, and with his own hammer and tool belt, he will be working on homes for low-income people in Indiana later this month. President Carter continues to live out his commitment to Jesus. You can too!

2) *The ex-missionary; bed ridden and committed.*

Many people have heard of Jimmy Carter. Fewer people know about Peg, who is one year younger and lives 1,500 miles west in Tucson, Arizona. And that's fine with her.

Peg devoted most of her life to serving the people of Africa as a Christian missionary. The work was hard, but she enjoyed it. Then, when she reached her late 60s, the work grew harder, and she came back to the U.S. She outlived many of her friends and family members, and now lives by herself in a room in a senior care facility. She is frail and failing.

At 93, Peg has some serious mobility issues, so she doesn't go out much. But even though she is nearing the end of her life, she isn't ending her ministry. She has found a way to serve God and share with others.

Most days, after settling back in bed after breakfast and a short walk, she settles in with A Tucson phone book, a magnifying glass to help her read the phone book, and a cell phone. Page by page and name by name, Peg is working her way through that phone book, calling people, saying hello, and asking them if they have experienced the love of God.

"Hi, I'm Peg, and I'm praying my way through the phone book. How may I pray for you?"

Some people hang up on her. Others politely sign off. But hundreds have talked with her, some for hours. As they pour out their hearts to Peg, she gives them her love and shares her wisdom about life.

Peg has found her own quiet, almost invisible way of sharing. She was called to serve others when she was in her 20s. Since then, her methods have changed but not her motivation. She's reaching out to strangers, helping them understand God's love and love Him back. She still has a vision.

I have a feeling Peg and Jimmy Carter would get along just fine. Both are still doing what they can to give what they have to people who need it. That's what the Sharing stage of retirement is all about.

One more example; Billy Graham wrote his last book at age 97. He wrote "Where I am: Heaven, Eternity, and Our Life Beyond" to show what God had taught him during the prior 97 years. You have a story too and it needs to be shared.

Primary Tasks of the Sharing Stage of Retirement

The end of life hasn't arrived yet, but people in the Sharing stage can certainly see it from where they are. The question is, what is everybody going to do about this profound reality?

My wife and I recently celebrated my 77th birthday with a few close friends. It was a nice evening, and our conversations showed me something important. Being able to see the end of life more clearly can bring a greater sense of peace with life and its varied circumstance.

I don't know if my kids are getting tired of hearing about all this, but I'm enjoying the chance to pass on a bit of the unique family that makes us who we are.

For example, my great grandfather left the Netherlands and came to the U.S. with three sons. He landed in Grand Rapids, Michigan with $3 in his pocket. He gave one dollar to the church, paid rent with the second dollar, and with the third dollar, he bought supplies to make cookies. He baked cookies, his sons sold cookies, and they ended up building a large family bakery, which provided a foundation for a later cracker company and a furniture company. I want my descendants to understand what you can do with a dollar, the entrepreneurial spirit, and hard work. I want that spirit living on in our family.

But remember: As you share these rich times with your loved ones, don't forget what's around the corner. You are not going to be present with these people forever.

These times together are your chance to acknowledge the shortness of time, express your love and affection, forgive past wrongs while seeking forgiveness for your own sins, and finding ways to say goodbye.

It's time for all of us to take stock. While thoughts about death and dying make many people fearful and anxious, followers of Christ don't need to feel that way. As we approach the end of our days, the Lord and Savior we have faithfully served stands ready to receive us into His heavenly kingdom. The closer we get to eternity, the less there is to fear.

It's like William Cowper says in "O for a Closer Walk with God," his classic hymn from the 1770s:

O for a closer walk with God,
a calm and heavenly frame,
a light to shine upon the road
that leads me to the lamb.

These were some of the sentiments we shared at my 77th birthday party. When we are closer to God life seems better and fuller. Our walk with God actually grows closer once we become acutely aware of the end of our brief time on earth. Our walk with God is closer when we grow our relationship with him, with Jesus, and our awareness of the Holy Spirit's role in our life. We can do our part to deepen that relationship through engaging with the words of Jesus in the Bible, talking to God though prayer, and being quiet in His presence.

Being anchored in a closer walk with God, brings comfort and stability, and promotes the growth of the fruits of the spirit: love, joy, peace, patience, kindness, gentleness and self-control. These attitudinal changes can keep people moving forward and using their bodies and brains to serve God during the decades of retirement. Walking closer with God leads us on His path and encourages us to demonstrate Jesus character to all me meet.

Your Homework Assignments for the Sharing Stage

It's a new stage of retirement, with its own unique list of assignments.

1) Finish Your Work.

"A record number of folks age 85 and older are working," reported *The Washington Post* in 2018.

"Nobody questions whether older workers can make a difference. After all, some of America's most prominent workers are around 85. The oldest Supreme Court justice, Ruth Bader Ginsburg, is <u>85</u>. Rupert Murdoch is <u>87</u>. So are George Soros, Warren Buffett and Toni Morrison."

The numbers the *Post* cited reveal significant changes. "Overall, 255,000 Americans 85 years old or older were working over the past 12 months. That's 4.4 percent of Americans that age, up from 2.6 percent in 2006, before the recession. It's the highest number on record."

Pastors are among those still working during the Sharing stage of retirement. Charles Swindoll, a bestselling author, famous radio preacher and pastor is 84. In addition to serving as Chancellor of Dallas Theological Seminary, Swindoll is the founding pastor of Stonebriar Church in Frisco, Texas.

Some people love working. Some people need to continue working. Whatever the reason, if you are working, finish your work. Do a good job. Conclude your long life of employment with your best work yet.

2) Kick back and relax.

On the other hand, if you've already worked hard for much of your life, now's the time for giving yourself permission to sit back, relax, and enjoy life's many blessings.

There are so many rich and wonderful things for you to enjoy during this stage of life: relationships, hobbies, learning, traveling, and more.

It's important you do these things rather than doing nothing, or passively absorbing television programming all the hours you are awake.

Continue to use your body and your mind, doing everything you can to keep both happy.

3) Escape the silo.

Have you noticed that as you have gotten older, so have many of the people around you? Social isolation can lead to depression. If you don't do something intentional to overcome the shrinking of your social circle, pretty soon old folks will be your only company.

The best response to this dead-end trend is finding ways to escape your social silo. Don't restrict your activities to one generational group but seek ways to make yourself generationally available. There are important roles you can play with those who are older and with those who are younger. Don't put yourself in a silo where you only see and socialize with your own age group.

4) Stay faithful at the end

This is the stage of life when your body and your mind may start ganging up on you in ways that you don't like very much. But don't give in to bitterness and despair. Thank God for the blessings He has given you and for long life well lived.

And the longer you are around, the more chances you have to observe your fellow human beings acting terribly, the exact opposite of a Christ follower. But don't give in to cynicism or close your heart to humanity. You're not perfect yourself, you know! You have been given the enormous amounts of grace, by God and everyone who knows you, much more grace than you realize or probably deserve. Continue showing that grace to all around you, rather than closing up on yourself.

When monks in medieval monasteries used the skulls of their deceased brethren as candlesticks holders, they weren't being morbid or disrespectful. They were acknowledging the reality of death and reflecting on that reality every day they were alive.

Christ has called us to be faithful for a lifetime, so stay faithful to the end. End well, with your love and faith intact. Continue to walk the path of wisdom, compassion, and love. This how God builds His Kingdom through us.

Embracing Your Stages of Retirement

Chances are that you weren't quite sure what I was talking about when I started explaining the three stages of retirement.

But now that we've explored the Active, Mentoring, and Sharing stages, I think you can see with me that retirement is not one homogenous, monolithic event. It's a series of seasons that may extend decades into your future.

No two retirement experiences are the same. Yours won't be the same as mine. People *do* seem to progress through these major stages of retirement, but at their own unique pace.

I've given you the broad outlines. Now it's your job to figure out where you are and start learning to address and embrace your particular place in this long and fascinating journey.

If you've ever wanted to be an opera singer, parachute out of an airplane at 30,000 feet, or write a great American memoir, sit down and start making your plans.

Questions for Reflection: There are Three stages of retirement outlined in the Chapter. List them here: Then note a person or couple you know who are in each stage

1. ?
2. ?
3. ?

1) Which of these three stages of retirement are you in right now? Or are you in the Preparation stage?

2) What are the main challenges and tasks for you during this stage of retirement? Or preparation?

3) One of the consistent themes through all three stages of retirement is the need to evaluate, develop and utilize your resources. But perhaps you have never thought about all the wisdom and insight you have built up over a lifetime. Take some time and write down the key gifts you have, both Natural and Spiritual. This analysis can help prepare you for developing and using these gifts during your next life-stage.

CHAPTER 10

THE POWER OF A PLAN

The bad news arrived in the summer of 2017. Sen. John McCain had developed brain cancer and would not have long to live.

For some people, such a diagnosis could lead to depression or grief. For McCain, the news meant it was time for him to get busy planning his future in two important ways. How he would live out the remaining months of his life? And how he would be publicly remembered after death?

Soon after he received the bad news, the Senator began convening weekly Friday meetings with his staff and aides to discuss and plan the many public events and memorial services that would pay tribute to his life of service. While aides reported that in these meetings McCain was dispassionate and down to business, some of the aides found these meetings so difficult that they retreated to a bar afterwards to commiserate and support each other.

McCain died on Saturday August 25, 2018, and over the following week, Americans could see his big plans play out.

- On Wednesday, which would have been his 82nd birthday, he lied in state in the Arizona State Capitol building, where there was a small private ceremony.
- On Thursday there was a service at North Phoenix Baptist Church, where former Vice President Joe Biden and other dignitaries gave tributes, followed by another private ceremony at Sky Harbor Airport attended by Arizona National Guard members.

- On Friday his body lay in state at the U.S. Capitol in Washington, D.C., an honor typically reserved for presidents.
- On Saturday, McCain's family escorted the former Marine's body to the Vietnam War Memorial, where they placed a wreath in his honor. Later that same morning there was a memorial service at the Washington National Cathedral, where eulogies were given by two ex-presidents who prevented McCain from reaching the White House himself: Republican George W. Bush and Democrat Barack Obama.
- On Sunday, after a final private ceremony at the U.S Naval Academy Cemetery in Annapolis, Maryland, the Senator was buried next to his longtime Navy buddy, Admiral Chuck Larson.

McCain was intimately involved in selecting all the speakers and musicians who participated in his memorial events. He personally chose the Irish song "Danny Boy" for the Arizona church service and called on old friends to serve as pallbearers, including actor Warren Beatty and FedEx founder Frederick W. Smith.

What's the Plan?

If I were to start giving out awards to people who planned their affairs so their lives would be full and end well, I would definitely give one of these awards to McCain. But unfortunately, I might not be able to hand out as many awards to other people as I would like to. That's because the vast majority of people don't do very much planning at all for the decades they may spend in retirement, their last final years of life, or how their deaths will be commemorated and celebrated.

The same weekend Americans were mourning the death of McCain, many of us were also grieving the death of Aretha Franklin, the Queen of Soul. Although her funeral arrangements were not as complicated as McCain's, she had done her homework, securing the services of former president Bill Clinton and other dignitaries from the worlds of music, religion and politics.

But after Franklin's funeral, there was sad news about the celebrated singer. She died without a will, meaning that her estimated $80 million estate would be subject to hefty probate taxes. Settling her affairs may ultimately involve legal challenges from family members, which could take years to resolve.

Franklin is far from alone. Many well-known entertainers lack even a basic will. Among those to die without wills were actor James Gandolfini, who played Tony Soprano in "The Sopranos."

Rock musician Prince died in 2016 with an estimated fortune of $200 million, but he didn't have a will. Two years later, lawyers and consultants have received millions of dollars in fees, but so far family members haven't seen a penny.

We may ask ourselves, "How could these people overlook such an important process?" But we should look in the mirror before we complain about others. According to one recent survey, nearly 60% of Americans have no will in place.

One national survey found that nearly 60% of Americans do not have a will.

A Plea for Planning

Millions of Americans have notebooks or files labeled "Retirement Planning." But there's more to retirement than money, and many people neglect to plan for how they will live life in retirement.

You may not be a celebrated politician or an entertainer with a multimillion-dollar estate, but no matter who you are, you must begin planning *now* for your remaining years.

How will you live?

How will you die?

How you will be remembered by loved ones and people you've known and worked with?

I know a man named Roger who retired from the military after 28 years of loyal service. His military job demanded detailed planning concerning the movement of troops and the resources those troops needed. It was demanding work, but he enjoyed it and found it stimulating.

I assumed Roger was the kind of person who would apply the same rigor to developing plans for how he would spend his retirement years. But as I found out one day, he didn't have a clue about his future.

"So, what's your plan?" I asked him one day after he announced his retirement.

"I don't know," he said. "I'm just going to take it step by step."

Roger had stored up significant financial resources, so he could afford to do pretty much whatever he wanted to do in retirement. But I was surprised to see that a man who had planned out so many details during his career years had suddenly "retired" from planning just as he was approaching retirement age. He had given little thought to what he wanted to do with his next 10, 20, or 30 years.

In recent months, I've connected with two other retirees who seem to be procrastinating instead of planning. The first is a 68-year-old executive who is about to retire after leading a major Christian ministry organization for more than 20 years. When I talked to him one day in the summer, it was five months before his upcoming retirement on December 31. He and the ministry's board were scrambling to find the right replacement, but the executive had given little thought to his own future.

"What are you going to do on January 1?" I asked him,

"I have no idea," he said.

"Have you even thought about it?"

"Not really," he said. "I've been too busy wrapping up my time here. I guess God will help me figure it out?"

If this man had gone to his board during the prior 20 years when he was leading the ministry, and if he had presented his board members with a similar lack of planning concerning some aspect of the ministry's future, they would not have been happy. If that was the way he handled ministry planning, it's likely he never would have lasted in his office for 20 years.

Yes, it's important to seek God's help in figuring out what to do in life. But inviting the Holy Spirit to guide you doesn't require you to throw up your hands and abrogate your responsibility in researching and choosing your best options.

Henrietta was the second procrastinating retiree I met. We both traveling on the same cruise ship. She was in her late 80's, and her husband had died more than 20 years earlier. He had worked as a physician and had retired 18 years prior to his passing. During those 18 years, the couple fulfilled their long-held dreams to travel extensively.

Henrietta told me that the two of them had planned one last, big, around-the-world trip, but her husband had suddenly become ill and was unable to take that trip with her. Just prior to his death he urged Henrietta to go ahead and take that trip without him, and that's exactly what she was doing.

I asked her what kind of planning she and her husband had done prior to his retirement. Her answer was typical of the answers I hear: "We did no real planning. It was more exciting that way."

When I asked her about the purpose of her life, she looked bewildered. "I have no idea about that," she said.

Preparing for the Inevitable

Everyone knows that time marches on, that tomorrow will be different from today, and that all of us should prepare ourselves for everything that's coming down the road for us, including old age and death. But are we ready for tomorrow?

The Wall Street Journal headline for June 22, 2018, gives a grim answer: "Time Bomb Looms for Aging America: A Generation of Americans Is Entering Old Age the Least Prepared in Decades."

"Americans are reaching retirement age in worse financial shape than the prior generation, for the first time since Harry Truman was president," said the article.

The article's numbers were numbing: "More than 40% of households headed by people aged 55 through 70 lack sufficient resources to maintain their living standard in retirement. That is around 15 million American households."

So, what gives? Why are today's retirees less prepared than earlier generations? There are a number of factors, but these two paragraphs from *The Wall Street Journal* story summarize one of the biggest shifts:

In the postwar era, for a while, fixed government and company pensions gave millions a guaranteed income on top of Social Security. An improving economy led to increased wages. Many Americans retired in better shape than their parents.

No more. Baby boomers were the first generation of Americans who were encouraged to manage their own retirement savings with 401(k)s and similar vehicles. Many made investing mistakes, didn't sock enough away or waited too long to start.

Some of you may remember the days when having a good job meant having good benefits, including an employee pension plan. "By the 1980s, 46% of private-sector workers were in a pension plan," said *The Journal*. Today, only 15% of workers have defined benefit pension plans with their employers, according to *The Economist*.

The rest of us are on our own. We know we're supposed to set up 401(k) or other types of self-funded retirement investments, and many of us did so. But few of us socked away the amounts of money needed to finance a lengthy retirement. And even those of us who did invest encountered problems when we unsuccessfully tried to pick the best stocks in our plans, or when the market declines of 2000 and 2008 wiped out major chunks of our savings. Then, we had to recover, which most of us did.

And as we saw in Chapter 5 ("The Longevity Revolution"), people are living longer, and that's complicating retirement.

"Gains in life expectancy, combined with the soaring price of education, have left people in their 50s and 60s supporting adult children and older relatives," said *The Wall Street Journal*.

The Senior Bankruptcy Boom

In the conversations I have with men and women who are either approaching or experiencing retirement, I hear many sorrowful confessions.

I feel like we are on our own, financially, with no one to really guide us or take care of us.

I still haven't gotten back to where I was during the so-called great recession of a decade ago.

We are just stretched way too thin.

Some of these men and women embody a disturbing trend: the rate of people 65 and older who are filing for bankruptcy is three times what was in 1991. This trend was reported in an August *New York Times* article headlined: "Bankruptcy Booms Among Older Americans as Safety Net Frays."

"For a rapidly growing share of older Americans, traditional ideas about life during retirement are being upended by a dismal reality: bankruptcy …

"Driving the surge is a three-decade shift of financial risk from government and employers to individuals, who are bearing an ever-greater responsibility for their own financial well-being as the social safety net shrinks." Unfortunately, way too many are doing "nothing" about this too.

Hundreds of thousands of Americans file for bankruptcy every year, and many of them hope filing will let them put the past behind them and give them a new chance for a brighter tomorrow. But when seniors declare bankruptcy, it's clearly more of a desperation move. Many of them realize they won't have the time to make things right and climb out of the financial hole they've dug for themselves.

What's the cause of all the financial strain? Pick your factors from the many listed in the *Times* article, which was based on a study by the Consumer Bankruptcy Project:

- Though responsibility for retirement has increasingly shifted to individuals, few people seem to have embraced that responsibility by socking away sufficient retirement savings.
- Medical expenses—either rising prices or one single unplanned procedure—can upset the apple cart and decimate people's savings.
- People are living longer, which means many retirees are still supporting or caring for older adults.
- Meanwhile, many seniors who have cosigned on their children's student loans now are responsible for paying back student debts of $60,000, $100,000, or more.

One legal expert summarized the challenges today's seniors face:
"They worked all of their lives, and did what they were supposed to do, and through circumstances like a late life divorce or a death of a spouse or having to raise grandkids, have put them in a situation where they are not able to make the bills."

Bruce Bruinsma

"It's a Sin to Plan"

Different people have different reasons for their failures to plan ahead. One of the most interesting reasons I've heard comes from Christians who say Christ wants them to wing it instead of "worrying about tomorrow." Some of them cite this passage from Jesus' sermon on the Mount:

"Therefore, I tell you, do not worry about your life, what you will eat or drink; or about your body, what you will wear. Is not life more than food, and the body more than clothes? Look at the birds of the air; they do not sow or reap or store away in barns, and yet your heavenly Father feeds them. Are you not much more valuable than they? Can any one of you by worrying add a single hour to your life?

"And why do you worry about clothes? See how the flowers of the field grow. They do not labor or spin. Yet I tell you that not even Solomon in all his splendor was dressed like one of these. If that is how God clothes the grass of the field, which is here today and tomorrow is thrown into the fire, will he not much more clothe you—you of little faith? So do not worry, saying, 'What shall we eat?' or 'What shall we drink?' or 'What shall we wear?' For the pagans run after all these things, and your heavenly Father knows that you need them. But seek first his kingdom and his righteousness, and all these things will be given to you as well. Therefore, do not worry about tomorrow, for tomorrow will worry about itself. Each day has enough trouble of its own (Matthew 6:28-34).

Remember the WWJD question: What Would Jesus Do? I've met more than my share of people who say they're sure Jesus would never plan. They think He just went wherever the Spirit sent him, moment by moment.

Jesus' Father is a planner extraordinaire. God laid out His plans for each one of us before the beginning of time. He planned to send His son, His ambassador, to demonstrate his love for us. It was a detailed plan, and Jesus meticulously carried out his part.

These believers forget that Jesus was a good planner. He was continually reminding His disciples of His coming crucifixion. And as he told them, "My Father's house has many rooms; if that were not so, would I have told you that I am going there to prepare a place for you?" (John 14:2).

The Bible is full of godly men and woman who planned and prepared for the future. David was a master of preparation from the days of his youth. His practice in using his slingshot during his years working as

108

a shepherd prepared him for his showdown with Goliath. Likewise, his musical practice prepared him to play the harp and singing for the troubled leader Saul. Later, David prepared Solomon for the construction of the temple, instructing him about the detailed design and the many exotic materials that would be needed.

Or look at the life of Moses. God planned that out, too. God had prepared Moses for his 40 years in the desert leading the people of Israel. That preparation came during Moses' earlier 80 years of pain, suffering, and slavery. When Pharaoh threatened to kill all of the male Hebrew children in Egypt, Moses was saved by being rescued into Pharaoh's house, thus preparing him for his later battles with the ruler.

And when the Israelites needed some moral clarity on how to live, God provided the Ten Commandments. God's plan for living was detailed and came with hand-delivery.

Or look at Noah. As the late Catholic Cardinal **Richard Cushing advised:** "Always plan ahead. It wasn't raining when Noah built the ark."

Finding God's Plan

Similar forms of preparation have happened in your life. Think of all the things you went through as a youngster, as a young adult, or as a middle-aged person. Think of everything you've experienced and learned.

Now, suddenly, you aren't required to work 40 or more hours a week any longer. Perhaps you retired, or sold your company, or decided to teach part time.

Now's your opportunity to put into motion the plan God had in mind for you from the dawn of time. God wants you to use all your experiences as he prepares you for something new and exciting you can do today and tomorrow. Now is your time to find out what this assignment is, because here you will find vision, purpose and joy!

What are those lessons and insights God has put into you, and what kind of meaningful work or service can you do in the future based on those tremendous gifts?

Answering that question gets to the heart of what I mean by retirement planning. Retirement planning doesn't stop with social security and 401(k)

s. Finding out what God wants you to do at this stage of your life is where the real planning for your future should start.

God has a plan for each of our lives, and His preparations for you and me have been underway since long before there was a you or a me. According to scripture, His plans for us have been in existence since before the dawn of Creation. At times, that concept can be difficult for me to wrap my mind around, but I take comfort in the fact that the all-knowing and all-powerful Creator of our cosmos puts time and effort into personally creating life-long development plans for you and me.

When Should I Start Planning for Tomorrow?

My military retiree friend Roger put off all retirement planning until he actually reached retirement. Hopefully you won't put it off that long.

Have you heard of a movement called FIRE that many millennial's claim is the answer to people's retirement challenges? FIRE stands for financial independence, retire early, FIRE movement cheerleaders say it's the only way to go. All you need is a large annual salary combined with low living expenses, allowing you to sock away more savings more quickly.

Some of the better-known FIRE retirees are high-tech workers making over $100,000 a year. The goal is to work hard for 10 or 15 years, invest $1 million or more, and then leave it all behind, retiring in your late 30s or early 40s, and living off investment returns of $40,000 or less per year. Some of the better-known FIRE retirees have left Silicon Valley for smaller towns (Bend, Oregon is popular and affordable), while others have bought tiny houses and moved to plots of land that are off the grid.

But why wait until your 30s or 40s to plan for retirement? Some financial advisors recommend that people start their retirement planning even earlier. Some experts say high school students stash away some of the money they earn from summer jobs in Roth IRA's, where all the money invested grow tax-free. (Parents have found that young people's interest in saving for retirement grows when mom and dad agree to match their children's savings.)

Fans of FIRE and enterprising high school students may plan far, far ahead. But most people aren't so focused. Fewer than a third of Americans are financially prepared. Fewer still seem prepared for *life* in retirement:

Me? Why? I'm never going to retire.

I'll die on the golf course (or as one pastor told me, *I'll die in the pulpit.*)

Now I have the time, but I don't have the money.

My wife says I need to go back to work.

My primary focus in life is groceries, doctors, and the dog.

Retirement is not in the Bible.

Retirement seems like a long time from now.

Retirement is an event that stretches to eternity.

I've worked all my life for this moment, and now that I'm not required to go to work, I don't really have anything to do.

I'm just going to keep working because there's not enough money.

Wise or Foolish?

Jesus knew His earthly ministry would last only a few years, and He repeatedly tried to explain to his disciples the many things to come. But his disciples didn't seem to understand. In Matthew 24 he told His disciples about the coming end of the age, the destruction of the Temple, and His own death. In Matthew 25 he tried to drive his points home with two parables: The Parable of the Ten Virgins and the Parable of the Talents.

Pastors often use The Parable of the Talents when they are preaching their stewardship sermons. A man is going on a journey, so he gives three of his servant's portions of his wealth. Two of the three servants traded and made even more money for their master, while the third servant hid the money in a hole in the ground. That made his master unhappy.

"You wicked and slothful servant! You ought to have invested my money with the bankers, and at my coming I should have received what was my own with interest. So, take the talent from him and give it to him who has the ten talents (Matthew 24:26-28).

The Parable of the Ten Virgins offers a similar message that focuses on the importance of planning:

At that time, the Kingdom of Heaven will be like the 10 Virgins who took their lamps and went out to meet the Bridegroom. Five of them were foolish and five of them were wise. The foolish ones took the lamps but did not take any oil with them. The wise ones took oil in their jars along with them (Mathew 25:14-30).

111

This parable is a stark reminder of those who presume that God will provide all of the resources needed to complete what He has called them to do. Don't get me wrong. God does provide, and most of the time He provides more than you and I want or deserve. But the Parable of the Ten Virgins shows us that God doesn't want us to wait on Him to provide when we are clearly capable of providing for ourselves.

The wise virgins not only brought oil, but they also had the jars needed to carry the oil. They did not merely fill up the bowl holding the wick, but also brought additional jars of oil as a back-up in case the night was long.

Why did these wise virgins plan like this? Perhaps they had faced similar oil problems before. Or perhaps they were blessed with the foresight to realize what would happen if they did not have enough.

Either way, these wise virgins were prepared. They were ready to wait a long time. They were spiritually prepared and could understand their relationship with the bridegroom. They even prepared to handle the problems caused by the foolish virgins.

Do you remember the old Sunday School song that goes like this?

"There is oil in my lamp,

Keep it burning, burning, burning.

There is oil in my lamp today!"

This could a powerful theme song for those of us who've never really gotten around to do the retirement and life planning that can make our futures as bright as a burning lamp.

Willing to Think About Tomorrow

When I talk to some people about planning, they try to use the "perfect plan" excuse on me: I don't want to work on a plan that's not perfect. That wouldn't be good for me!"

Military genius **George S. Patton addressed that phobia with this simple rejoinder:**

"A good plan today is better than a perfect plan tomorrow."

Do you have a good plan for your future years?

If so, congratulations. I can now award you one of the same awards I wanted to give to John McCain.

If not, why not?

In the next section of this book, we will walk you through all the issues and challenges you need to consider as you make your retirement plans. All you need to do is follow up and do the work.

Are you willing to spend a few hours today in planning for a better tomorrow?

Are you willing to pray and seek God's will for the remaining years of your life?

Are you willing to read books and attend workshops so you can be better informed and better prepared for everything that's coming?

Are you willing to take one step, then another, and another, as you journey into a life of retirement?

If so, please join me in the final chapters of the book.

If not, get ready for to find out what the consequences of poor preparation look like.

Questions for Reflection

What is the downside of not planning?

What is the downside of not listening to God's plan?

1) Many people do "retirement planning" when it comes to their finances, but they fail to do equally robust planning when it comes to how they will spend, invest, their lives in retirement. For a moment, forget about money and finances and answer these questions:

   a) What do I most want to do most in retirement?

b) What do I need to do most in retirement?

c) What are some other activities I would like to do or goals I would like to achieve in retirement?

d) What do I want to achieve with my spouse, my family, during retirement?

e) How do I want to impact other people during retirement?

f) What's on my "bucket list"?

g) What do I sense God calling me to do during retirement?

SECTION 3

THE RETIREMENT REFORMATION: CHANGING HOW WE LIVE, SAVE, AND WORK

CHAPTER 11

GETTING TO RETIREMENT

After nearly 50 movies in 60 years, Academy Award-winner Robert Redford said his 2018 film, "The Old Man & the Gun," would be his last as leading man.

"You know, I can't do this forever," Redford told CBS Sunday Morning. "I've been doing it since I was 21. As you move into your 80s, you say, 'Hey, that's enough, that's enough.'"

Redford says he will likely continue working in the industry, but his days as leading man are now over. That's his way of getting to retirement.

What's your way of getting to retirement? You may not be a world-famous actor deciding whether or not to do another movie. Perhaps you are an employee trying to figure out how long to continue working. Or perhaps you're a small business owner wondering how long you want to keep running your company.

Retirement is coming for all of us. The big question for you is: What form will retirement take in your life?

The answer to that question depends on many factors, but the most important factor is you, your preparation, passion and relationship with God.

What form will retirement take in your life? The answer to that question depends on many factors, but the most important factor is you.

What is your goal in retirement?

What is your ongoing mission?

What is God's preferred plan for your future?

How long have you been preparing to retire?

And when will those preparations allow you to join with Robert Redford in saying, "Hey, that's enough"?

You've seen thousands of advertisements warning you to prepare for retirement, but 99% of those advertisements equate preparation with financial planning. As we've seen, there's much more to retirement planning than financial planning. Money is important, but you also have a life to live. How will you plan that life in retirement?

Let's see what it means to be prepared for retirement *in many ways*: financially, physically, emotionally, and spiritually.

The Retirement Savings Landscape: The View from 30,000 feet

"Find a need and fill it." The late Robert Schuller offered this nugget of professional advice during one of his televised sermons from the Crystal Cathedral. I was watching when he said it, and the timing could not have been better for me.

It was the 1970s, and I was in my 40s. I was uncertain about where my career path would take me. That's when my future fell into my lap, thanks to the U.S. government.

History was made in the late 1970s when a group of highly paid American executives approached members of Congress with a request. The executives wanted to invest part of their earnings in the stock market, and they wanted Congress to help them out by changing American tax laws to exempt those investments from income taxes.

Congress obliged. When legislators passed the Revenue Act of 1978, they created a new bonus for investors found in section 401(k) of the Internal Revenue Code.

The executives made their investments and received their exemptions, but hardly anyone else noticed or understood what this new legislation had done until two years later. In 1980, a financial consultant named Ted Benna realized that the new 401(k) legislation provided and incentive for many Americans—not only highly paid executives—to save for retirement and save on taxes.

Employees of Benna's company were the first in America to enjoy a company provided 401 plans. Then in 1981, the IRS issued new rules allowing companies to fund employees' 401(k) plans through payroll deductions. The IRS also made it easier for people to create individual retirement arrangements, or IRAs.

I had a feeling that 401(k)s and IRAs would revolutionize retirement savings in America, and I wanted to be in the forefront of the revolution. But I wasn't sure about the long-term career prospects, so I set up meetings with three respected business leaders and asked them two big questions.

"Do you think these new investment vehicles will have a big impact?" I asked in my first question.

"Yes, absolutely," they said. "This will be huge."

My second question for my three experts was more complicated, and more personal. Because my parents had been college instructors, and my wife Judy worked as a third-grade public school teacher, I had a passion for helping teachers and other people who worked in schools plan and save for their financial futures. (Instead of using 401(k)s, teachers, ministers and employees of tax-exempt organizations use 403(b)s to save for retirement.)

"So, do you think I can carve out a career serving the people that use 403(b)s?"

"Absolutely not," replied my three business leaders. "It just won't work. For one thing, these people don't earn as much money as those employed in the private sector. As a result, saving is not their priority. In addition, many of the schools and non-profits who employ them are small organizations that offer lower pay."

If I had been making a purely financial decision based on how much I thought I could earn throughout my career, I would have stayed away from teachers and religious workers with their 403(b)s, and focused solely on people with 401(k)s. But I followed my intuition, launching a new company that helped teachers, administrators, janitors, and others who worked in public schools. It was counter-intuitive, yet I figured there had to be a way for people with normal, middle-class jobs and incomes to save for retirement. If nobody else wanted to do it, there must be a need and an opportunity.

Later, after my journey to Timbuktu (see Chapter 6), I applied the same approach to pastors, missionaries, and other religious leaders. Today, Envoy Financial helps thousands of churches, ministries and leaders use 403(b) plans to save for retirement and beyond.

I proved the skeptical business leaders wrong, helping thousands and thousands of people of faith plan and save and prepare for retirement by finding a need and filling it.

I am still pleased to receive that unique calling and am grateful to play a role in helping people change the course of their financial lives. But I continually ran into two huge challenges that I call the What? Problem and the Why? Problem.

- ***The What? Problem*** focuses on savings. The problem is that everyone should save for retirement, but not everyone does so, and even many who do save for retirement don't save as much as they should. The financial services industry operates on the assumption that if people knew how to invest, they would save more. The results over the last 30 show the industry is wrong and starting with wrong assumptions.
- ***The Why? Problem*** focuses on not on savings but on living. The Why? problem involves deeper issues of life. Why are you retiring? What kind of life do you hope to experience during retirement? What will life look like? What meaning will you find in those upcoming years? So many retirees focus on what they are leaving (typically, years of work) that they expend little effort looking ahead to what their newfound freedom will look like.

The What? And Why? problems are related. For example, if you fail to plan and don't save anything for retirement, your plans for retirement will be simple: Keep on working. Today many people work well into their 70s and 80s to make up for their lack of planning and saving. But it doesn't need to be that way.

If you focus on both the What? and Why? problems, you can improve the trajectory of your life in retirement.

The What? Problem: People Don't Save

It has been nearly forty years since Congress gave Americans the 401(k) and the IRA to help them save for retirement. So, what hath this legislation wrought? As of June 2018, 401(k) plans held more than $5 trillion in assets, while IRAs held more than $7 trillion in assets.

These vast numbers make it seem like everyone is saving for retirement, but nearly a quarter of Americans have saved nothing, according to an article on the CNBC website.

"When it comes to retirement savings, Americans know they are falling behind — and it's stressing them out," said the article.

Evidence of stress was found in Northwestern Mutual's "2018 Planning & Progress" study. The study found that 78 percent of Americans say they're "extremely" or "somewhat" concerned about not having enough money for retirement. Another 66 percent are concerned that they'll outlive their retirement savings.

Others simply ignore the issue altogether until it's too late. Some of these late-starters encourage themselves with the words of the little engine that could: "I think I can. I think I can." But maxims can't make up for failing to put a sustainable plan into motion earlier on.

The Why? Problem: People Don't Know Their Purpose in Retirement

So, what *should* we spend our lives doing, and why is it important? This purpose question is more crucial than questions about finances and savings, even though fewer people ask it. Many think about financing retirement—even people who aren't saving. But not many consider their purpose in retirement. They know that working and earning were the goals of their career years, but when those activities disappear, the need for a purpose continues.

Why are we alive?

What is our purpose in living today and for the decades to come?

Many people think about financing retirement, but fewer even consider their purpose in retirement.

Your financial planner can't answer your questions about meaning and purpose. Those answers need to come from other sources. As we saw earlier, the Westminster Catechism says: "Man's chief end is to glorify God, and to enjoy him forever."

Scripture gives us additional guidance about our purpose in life. Paul explains that God has different purposes for each of us:

In a large house there are articles not only of gold and silver, but also of wood and clay; some are for special purposes and some for common use. Those who cleanse themselves from the latter will be instruments for special purposes, made holy, useful to the Master and prepared to do any good work (2 Timothy 2:20-21).

You and I were created by God to be instruments for His special purposes, purposes that we may not have been aware of during our hectic years of work and career. But as we move through each of life's stages, we have fresh opportunities to prepare for the future, live with less chaos, grow spiritually, listen for God's guidance, and find our higher purpose.

The Retirement Savings Landscape: The View from Where You Are

Trillions of dollars are invested in 401(k) and IRA accounts. Are you one of those people who have saved well? How financially prepared are you for retirement? We will explore this big question with four smaller questions on your income and assets, expenses, debts, and spending patterns.

Money may not be the most important piece of the retirement puzzle but having too little of it tends to direct our paths. Here are some helps to think about your financial landscape and the options you have:

Your Income and Assets

Do you own a house or other real property?

Do you currently receive income from a job? If not, can you do so?

What about vehicles? Do you have a car, boat, or RV that's rarely used?

Do you have other forms of income: tax refunds, alimony, Social Security, inheritance, trust, or will?

Cool Tool: The Retirement Income Calculator from T. Rowe Price can help you get a better handle on your projected monthly income in retirement. (See TRowePrice.com)

Another Cool Tool: The Social Security Benefits Calculator helps you understand your benefits and determine your best timeframe for starting to receive those benefits. For example, when you become eligible for Social Security, your spouse is also eligible for at least 50% of your benefit amount. (AARP.org)

Your Expenses

How is your spending? Is it budgeted and controlled, or freewheeling?

How much do you spend compared to how much you earn: Spend less? About the same? Spend more?

Is your spending prioritized? Do you cover obligations and needs before spending on wants?

Are there areas of hidden spending that you overlook or minimize? Do you spend more than you think on eating out, gift giving, or dry cleaning?

Cool Tool: The Projected Retirement Expense Calculator from the California Teachers Association is a good tool for estimating expenses during every year of your retirement. (CTAinvest.org)

Your Debts and Liabilities

Are you carrying a loan on your home or car?

Do you have student debts you are paying off?

Your Savings

Do you save?

Are you currently investing in your financial future through an IRA, or 401(k), employer pension, or other forms of retirement savings?

Q: So, when should I start saving for retirement?
A: Yesterday, or sooner.

I have good news for the millions of Americans who have done little or nothing to prepare financially for retirement: ***It's never too late to start.***

I have even better news for the millions of are younger Americans who are not saving for retirement: ***It's never too early to start.*** Let me show you why.

I have good news for the millions of Americans who have done little or nothing to prepare financially for retirement: *It's never too late to start.* I have even better news for the millions of are younger Americans who are not saving for retirement: *It's never too early to start.*

Joe is 25, and Joanne is 35. Both work for the same company. Neither previously had a retirement savings account, but both are starting one today. Let's see how that decade difference in their ages will impact their savings by the time they reach retirement.

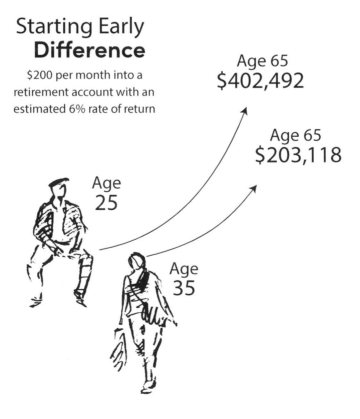

Starting Early
Difference

$200 per month into a retirement account with an estimated 6% rate of return

Age 65
$402,492

Age 65
$203,118

Age 25

Age 35

Joe and Joanne both elected to have their employer deduct $200 from their monthly salary and place it in a retirement savings account. Both will continue with these monthly deductions until they retire at the age of 65.

That's when the wisdom of starting early will show up. By the time Joanne retires, after 30 years of work and deductions, she will have accumulated just over $200,000 in retirement savings.

Meanwhile Joe, who will have been saving the same monthly amount for 40 years, will leave work with just over $400,000 in retirement savings. Joe's 10-year head start results in a retirement savings account that's worth twice as much as Joanne's. (Note: This comparison assumes their savings accounts earned an estimated 6% annual rate of return.)

The moral of the story is clear:

- Start saving yesterday, or sooner, if possible.
- If you're just now starting to save, some is better than none, and a little is better than nothing.

A Plan for Every Age and Stage

Failing to plan means planning to fail. I know some people will say that's a cliché, but it's not a cliché to me because I see it happen every day. Let's face facts:

- Someday you will retire or, your work will end, or change dramatically.
- Because of longer life expectancy, you may live two or three decades after age 65 or even 70 in retirement.
- Living costs money.

Planning for retirement is not a one-size-fits-all situation. Different people have different needs and assets. There is one other important difference: Planning for retirement changes as we move through the stages of life. Men and women who are just starting their careers and families deal with financial demands that can make it difficult for them to save. On the other hand, people who are nearing the end of their working careers typically can set more aside for the future.

But those just starting out shouldn't ignore planning and saving for retirement. Like everyone, they need to do what's appropriate for their stage. A little early can grow to sufficient later.

Let's look at the three life stages and describe the retirement planning assignments for each stage.

Life Stage 1) Just Starting Out: 20s and 30s

You may be young, but that's no excuse to ignore tomorrow. Embrace this time as chance to put your future on a firmer foundation.

You may be young, but that's no excuse to ignore tomorrow.

As people launch their careers and start their families, income is probably lower than it will be in the future, and expenses may be proportionately higher.

Therefore, your primary goal in this stage isn't to stash away millions of dollars (although that would be nice). The main goal here is to be as financially savvy as you can by avoiding some of the ill-considered mistakes young people make, often because they are unaware of the consequences.

Exhibit A hits close to home. It is a perfect example of one of the dumbest decisions I made as a young, unenlightened husband.

Judy and I were married and living in California. I was studying at the University of California, Berkeley, hard at work on an MBA. Meanwhile, Judy was hard at work teaching third grade in the San Leandro School District.

We lived in a small apartment, and were very careful with our spending. Over time Judy was able to build a small retirement fund through the school district. Once I finally graduated, we were off to Dearborn, Michigan for my new job with the Ford Motor Company.

There was only one problem: Our new Michigan home had no furniture. Judy made a suggestion and I wholeheartedly went along: Let's cash out those retirement funds, pay the taxes for early withdrawal, and use what's left to buy ourselves some furniture for our new home.

That's what we did, but do you know what? If we had kept that money in Judy's retirement account, it could be worth $50,000 or more today. In retrospect, that furniture turned out to be *very* expensive. It cost us $50,000 and we have none of it today—neither the money nor the furniture.

Learn your lesson from me. If you're just starting out, don't jeopardize your future by making unwise decisions about your retirement accounts or any other assets. Stop and think first.

Here are a few other things to remember as you are starting out.

- Start saving now. If your employer offers one, enroll in a pretax 403 (b), 457, or 401(k) defined contribution plan, and see if your employer offers matching contributions.
- If you can set aside additional income, create a Roth IRA and fund it with a monthly contribution.
- If you have student debts, pay them off, but not so quickly that you lose available tax deductions for interest on your loans.
- Buying your own house may take time. Begin by siphoning off cash for a down payment every month. And don't get in over your head when you do make that purchase. Here is the long-term view, own your house free and clear when you hit 65.

Life Stage 2) Picking Up Speed: 40s to mid 50s

It may have been difficult for you to save much for retirement during your 20s and 30s, but now that you are in your 40s and 50s, it's time for you to get serious. The longer you neglect to save for retirement, the more likely it is you will face financial challenges in the years ahead.

The money we save for retirement doesn't merely sit there. It is invested. Three variables determine how much those investments will grow:

- How much you save and invest (your savings amount).
- How quickly your assets multiply (the rate of return on your investments).
- How long your assets can grow before you retire (the time value of money).

In my retirement planning workshops, I ask people to rank these three variables in order of importance. Typically, Arguments ensue as people debate what's most important. As the debate heats up, I chime in to settle the argument. The most important factor to growing your retirement savings is time. The amount you invest is important. The rate of return on your investments is important. But as we saw in our comparison of Joe and Joanne, time trumps all.

An analysis by T. Rowe Price explained the problem this way:

- If you start saving for retirement in your 20s, you only need to save 13% of what you earn.
- If you wait until you are 40 to start saving, you will need to sock away 26 to 29% of your salary to catch up.
- Things are worse if you wait until age 55. If you start saving for retirement at this late stage and you will need to save 43% of your earnings.

Some people look at this analysis and get depressed. I say, "Don't get depressed, get going!" And once you get going, keep going. That's the key: not stopping.

Government leaders realize that people don't always do what they should, so Americans are given powerful incentives to save for retirement once they are 50 years old. These "catch-up" incentives allow older people to put away larger amounts in their IRAs and retirement plans than younger people.

This analysis demonstrates *the power of compounding*, which happens when the dollar you invest earns you five cents of interest, and this interest is reinvested, increasing the size of your nest egg.

Americans are impatient people who want things to go fast. But this emphasis on speed prevents many people from embracing a long-term approach to their financial futures.

Here's an intriguing question I ask my seminar groups: Which would you rather have, a check for $200,000 right now, or the value of a penny, doubled daily, for 30 days?

Most people go for the $200,000 check, but in doing so they are losing millions. I've done the math so you can see the results for yourself. If you received one penny on day one, two pennies on day two, and continued this pattern for 30 days, you would walk away with $5,368,708.80.

How Assets Grow Over Time

If you take a penny and double its value every day for 30 days, you will be a wealthy person! This model shows the power of compounding.

Day 1: 1 cent
Day 2: 2 cents
Day 3: 4 cents
Day 4: 8 cents
Day 5: 16 cents
Day 6: 32 cents
Day 7: 64 cents
Day 8: $1.28
Day 9: $2.56
Day 10: $5.12
Day 11: $10.24
Day 12: $20.48
Day 13: $40.96
Day 14: $81.92
Day 15: $163.84
Day 16: $327.68
Day 17: $655.36
Day 18: $1,310.72
Day 19: $2,621.44
Day 20: $5,242.88
Day 21: $10,485.76
Day 22: $20,971.52
Day 23: $41,943.04
Day 24: $83,886.08
Day 25: $167,772.16
Day 26: $335,544.32
Day 27: $671,088.64
Day 28: $1,342,177.20

Day 29: $2,684,354.40
Day 30: $5,368,708.80

Most of us aren't too excited about the first ten days, but things get more exciting in days 25 to 30. The lesson is simple: You can't have the results of day 30 without day 1.

The Power of Time

Time is powerful. That's why you need to start saving now. Here are a few other priorities to keep in mind during your 40s and 50s:

- Prepare for contingencies by creating an emergency fund that can cover 3 to 6 months of basic expenses.
- Plan wisely for your children's college educations by starting a college savings fund early. (Other options include giving birth to kids who are really smart, really athletic, or both. You can also save by starting out with two years at a local or community college before transferring to a major academic institution.
- Watch out for weddings. A father I know asked for my advice. How could he fund his daughter's upcoming wedding? I asked how much the wedding would cost, and alarm bells started going off in my mind as soon as he said $100,000. Worse yet, his plan for coming up with the necessary funding involved borrowing $50,000 from a bank and taking a $50,000 loan against his retirement plan. I cautioned him about both the exorbitant cost of the wedding and his proposed method of funding. He went ahead with the plan, perceiving that his only daughter deserved such extravagance. Seven months later, I saw my friend again. He was not happy to see me. His daughter and her husband were divorcing, and he still owed the $100,000. The key is simple: Put realistic boundaries on what you are able and willing to contribute to the wedding. If the kids want to spend more, it's from their resources not yours.
- Contribute as much as you can to your retirement savings, at least 10% of your gross income. And if you get to the end of the year

and have some cash left over, invest even more. The key is this: First comes the Kingdom of Heaven, and then all your earthly savings can be supported. God guides our living, plus our giving.

Life Stage 3) Getting Closer: 55 to Retirement

Retirement may not have arrived quite yet, but you can probably see it from here! How do you feel as this next season of life comes into view?

If you are anything like the composite figures that emerge from detailed studies by Envoy Financial and many other groups, I have a hunch about what you may be feeling.

If you are part of the 22% of Americans who have saved $250,000 or more for retirement, you may have mixed feelings. You are glad you've saved more than many people you know, but you also realize that everything you have saved probably won't be enough for a lengthy retirement.

You are probably feeling worse if you are among the 33% of Americans who have put away less than $10,000 for retirement. If you are in your 20s, $10,000 is a good start. If you are in your 50s, get ready to keep working and earning.

As we saw in Chapter 7, retirement is complicated and forces you to answer complex questions about where you will live, who you will associate with, and what you will do. As you enter this third Life Stage, there are major decisions you can make that can substantially improve your retirement options.

Here are six wise steps you can take.

- Put away as much as you can while you can. For many men and women, their 50s and 60s are prime earning years. Make the most of these years by adding as much as you can to your retirement savings.
- Dare to downsize. Moving to a smaller, less expensive home can save you thousands of dollars a year in mortgage payments, maintenance, utilities, insurance, and taxes.
- Carefully weigh your Social Security options. Delaying your start date for benefits can vastly increase your long-term financial future.

- Consolidate your plans. People who work for different employers in different states can accumulate a number of different retirement accounts. Work with a qualified tax accountant and your financial planner to consolidate your plans into one plan that is attuned to your current and future needs.
- Consider long-term care insurance. This industry continues to change so much that it's difficult to offer actionable advice in a book. You can explore whether this option works for you. Examine and compare various long-term care products, applying their financial formulas to your unique life circumstances. (Remember that the average male needs special care for 18 months, while the average female approximately three years of care.)
- Try it on for size. You don't need to guess how much money it will take you to live in retirement. Instead of guessing, try an experiment. Try living on your projected retirement income for six months while you are still working. I guarantee this experience will help you refine your numbers.

Don't be like the people who see retirement as one of those big, 3,000-piece puzzles that can cover a table top. They see how the puzzle *should* look by looking at the photo on the box, but they have no idea how to assemble all 3,000 pieces into a coherent picture.

Start putting your retirement puzzle pieces together now, or you may spend your future overwhelmed by thousands of tiny pieces that don't fit together.

People take various routes to retirement, and only you can decide which route makes the most sense for you. As you reflect on your options, ask yourself which route will best serve God's plans for you, and which route gives you meaning and purpose in life?

Remember: Retirement is not only *freedom from* the obligations of the past. More importantly, it is *freedom to do* the things you've been waiting to do.

Questions for reflection:

1. Describe your "money" position

    a. Good

    b. Bad

    c. So, so

    d. Don't know

2. What changes, if any, do you need to make to address this money issue?

3. Am I on the same page as my spouse about money?

CHAPTER 12

BEYOND MONEY TO MEANING

Experts in the field of human survival talk about the "rule of threes." We can live without food for about three weeks. We can survive without water for about three days. But death comes after only three minutes without oxygen.

These are the requirements of biological survival. But there's more to human life than biology. Jesus fasted 40 days and nights in the desert and was tempted by Satan. At the end of His ordeal, He didn't talk about food or water, but something deeper.

"It is written: 'Man shall not live on bread alone, but on every word that comes from the mouth of God'" (Matthew 4:4).

What's the purpose of life? Here's how a varied group of wellness experts and authors answered the question.

"I believe that the very purpose of life is to be happy," wrote the Dalai Lama. "From the very core of our being, we desire contentment. In my own limited experience, I have found that the more we care for the happiness of others, the greater is our own sense of well-being."

Other authors cited in the article said purpose in life could be found through exploring life and experiences, or self-actualization, or living mindfully and passionately.

Minimalist guru Joshua Becker, who convinced his family to give away 70% of their possessions so they could live a simpler lifestyle, said, "The purpose of life is to give it away in the service of others."

None of the contributors suggested that gathering and saving money was the purpose of life. That's interesting, because I know many people (and financial planners) who act as if money is the most important element in preparing for retirement.

Don't get me wrong. Money is an important asset, both for those who have it and those who don't.

Money can provide a type of earthly security. It can provide us with the flexibility we need to respond to new opportunities and challenges. Money can stabilize our lives. It can give us the freedom to make choices that aren't limited or determined by our need for financial necessities.

Meanwhile, a lack of money will focus millions of people spending their later years working for needed income rather than experiencing some of the other things they hoped to do. Rather than finally accomplishing some of the things they are called to do, activities bringing them joy and a feeling of personal accomplishment, they're still working for the basic resources needed to survive. The freedom to find meaning and purpose is a treasure.

Money is important, but it isn't everything. Many people have more than enough financial assets to support them throughout retirement but lack any sense of deeper meaning or purpose in life.

But money isn't everything. I have met many people who have more than enough monetary assets to support them throughout retirement, but they lack a sense of deeper meaning or purpose in life beyond leisure, travel, hobbies, or warming a familiar spot on the couch.

If I were to take Jesus' comment on bread, and tweak it to address the realities of retirement in the 21st century, it might go something like this:

"Older men and women shall not live on bridge or shuffleboard alone, nor by early bird meals alone, nor by leisure and recreational activities alone. But they shall find joy and contentment by finding their meaning and purpose during these last seasons of life and pursuing their meaning and purpose with everything they have."

Living in Limbo

Many retirees I meet seem to be living in a weird state of limbo. Their bodies are here in the present, but their minds are focused somewhere back in the past (perhaps because we lose our short-term memory first but retain details from years ago).

When I ask them about who they are and what they care about, many of them seem to be grieving the loss of the identity from earlier decades:

I used to have an important, well-paying job, but now I'm retired.

I used to raise kids, but now I'm retired.

Listening between the lines, I hear many people making this sorrowful confession:

I used to do something. My life used to mean something. I had an identity. But now that I'm retired, I no longer do much of value. And I'm not sure what my meaning is any more.

They remind me of F. Scott Fitzgerald's description of Tom, the former football star:

"(Tom), among various physical accomplishments, had been one of the most powerful ends that ever-played football at New Haven—a national figure in a way, one of those men who reach such an acute limited excellence at twenty-one that everything afterward savors of anti-climax."

Most did not even think about meaning or purpose after retirement decades ago, because the duration of retirement was short. Today, people are spending 10, 20, or even 30 years in retirement. If that sounds like a terribly long time to live without a purpose, you're right. God prepares us to do good work, to continue to reflect Jesus, resulting in an understanding of our meaning and purpose. There is growing evidence that meaning and purpose are essential elements of a healthy and happy life, especially in retirement.

You don't need to believe me. Google the subject and read some of the startling headlines:

"Rise in Elderly Suicides: A Crisis of Meaning"

"Baby Boomers: From Great Expectations to a Crisis of Meaning"

"Factors Facilitating the Meaning Crisis in the Elderly: A Qualitative Study"

"The Nurture of the Elderly: Aging and the Crisis of Meaning"

When I talk to groups about living all of life with purpose and meaning, the questions come fast and furious:

Is there really a purpose for me beyond rest and relaxation?

What can I do?

Where can I find meaning in my daily existence?

Is it possible I have a purpose in life that no one else can fulfill but me?

If so, how can I figure out what it is?

Or is it already too late for me to get started?

No, it's not too late. Our longer lifespans give us more time to seek and live out our purpose in life. If you are still breathing, you have a purpose in life.

More people are discovering a powerful blessing that shows up during retirement: This a perfect time to reflect and reconnect with your purpose. You can experience the blessing that comes from being connected to God's plan for your whole life.

When the paychecks stop, the kids have grown and moved on, and it's just you and your spouse living out your days, this may be your optimal time for finding and fulfilling your purpose. Each stage of retirement has a purpose. Experience the joy by fulfilling it.

So, what is *your* purpose? Only you can tell, but here are some of the ways others have sought to live their retirement years with purpose, meaning, and joy.

Pursuing Purpose: Living with Intentionality

Prior to retirement, many people live divided lives. Working people divide their lives into two categories: What is needed for their jobs and careers, and what they choose to do when their time is their own to spend on family, recreation, or hobbies.

In retirement, there's neither a boss or supervisor prioritizing your activities nor a business requiring a prescribed regimen Your 9am to 5pm, or 8am to 8pm were not your own. With a smile, a friend confided to me that he just traded one boss at work for another one at home. You now have the luxury tinged with a bit of fear looking at the boss in the mirror every morning. This new boss can be confused, demanding, or just disconnected.

The problem is: Too many retired people never take on the job of being their own boss in retirement. They passively drift along through their last few decades of life instead of accepting the challenge to find and follow their purpose. It's all part of preparation, knowing what's coming next and embracing it with a smile.

In retirement, the only boss is you. But too many retired people never take on the job of being their own boss in retirement. They passively drift along through their last few decades of life instead of accepting the challenge to find and follow their purpose.

Do you want to live with meaning and purpose? Then live with intentionality. Use your newfound freedom from work as an opportunity to live out your ongoing purpose. Be deliberate rather than letting other people or circumstances call the shots.

Let's look at one area where living with intentionality reaps huge rewards: Relationships.

In the past, work and other obligations limited the time and energy you had to invest in relationships with family, friends, and other loved ones. Now that you are freed from these limitations, you can devote more time to intentionally investing yourself in the people in your life. Here is your chance to focus on emotional growth and maturity, and to speak wisdom and healing into some of the troubled relationships in your life.

Each and every one of us has some type of troubled relationship. Emotional maturity equips us to deal with those issues, and to do it with love.

Thanks to the gifts of retirement and longevity, you have more opportunity than any previous generation to spend quality time with the people you love. Don't miss this chance to connect with loved ones. With advanced technology you can spend quality time with others even though you're thousands of miles apart. Embrace the opportunity.

You have more energy for activities and outings now that you don't work 40 or more hours per week. You will inevitably slow down a bit as the years pass, so make the time count.

You are less stressed and preoccupied, which means you can devote more time to practicing key conversational techniques such as deep listening and honoring what people say.

Perhaps you've been involved with your children and grandchildren over the years. Now is your time to get more involved. Not only is grandparenting fun, but it can be a powerful way to leave a positive legacy. When you love your grandchildren, you are not only blessing them. You are also blessing their parents, and you are blessing future generations through your investment of time and love.

Grandparenting is more complicated than most suppose. Read a book, take a class, learn from others and you will reap even greater grandparenting rewards than you thought possible.

Living with intentionality applies to even the simplest and most basic parts of life. When you go to a store or the post office, try a little kindness. Instead of merely conducting your transactions and rushing out the door, take a few seconds to acknowledge and bless the people who are serving you. You've undoubtedly experienced bad service. Now praise those who give you good service.

One of the most satisfying ways to live with intentionality is by investing yourself in activities or causes that you never even considered before because you simply didn't have the time. Now's your chance to keep an open mind and discover what role you can play in helping others.

Maybe you have always wanted to use your mind more, but in the past, you didn't have quality time or energy for reading. Now you do, and perhaps your enjoyment can grow by joining a book group and discussing books with others.

Reading books or listening to audiobooks can bring a lifetime of enjoyment, so start as soon as you can. I've discovered that listening to books through services such as Audible is an easy way to get back in the learning groove.

Maybe you have been a pew-sitter at church for too long. Here's your chance to sing in the choir, or join a prayer or study group to take you deeper in your faith, or get involved in serving your brothers and sisters in the body of Christ.

There are a million things you can choose. What makes the most sense for you? How has God prepared you, and what are you ready for next?

Whatever you do don't forget to plan activities that are exciting, world-enlarging, and life-giving. During your decades of work, did you ever daydream at your desk or in your car about simple, fun things you would like to enjoy? Here's your chance.Help others, love yourself, reflect Jesus in all you do.

A Handy Model for Life Purpose: WWJD

Do you remember the WWJD movement, which we discussed in Chapter 10? For a few years it seemed like many people focused on this simple but profound question: What Would Jesus Do?

As I talk to people in retirement about living lives of meaning and purpose, I have found that many men and women can find plenty of purposeful things to do by studying Christ's life and ministry. He packed a lot into His three years of ministry. There is much there to challenge and encourage us.

Notice, the question isn't: What would Jesus preach? Talk can be cheap, and it's sinfully easy to stand apart from and condemn the world's evil without getting personally involved.

Instead, your emphasis should be on action, on doing, on rolling up your sleeves and diving into other people's complex and often messy lives. Our actions speak louder and reach deeper than mere words. The truth of God's love is sometime best expressed through His servants' gracious service to others.

After you've helped someone, how do you feel? If you are encouraged, do it some more. It may lead to your new pathway.

How can you act in ways that are consistent with Jesus' will for you? His call is to bear fruit that will last (John 15:8). Here are two practical suggestions you can find by reading the New Testament and looking for assignments.

Love your neighbor. Jesus told his followers to love God and love their neighbors. (Mark 12:30-31). Do you have neighbors? People who live next door to you, but who you have perhaps never really talked to?

Now, in this new phase of your life, you can love these people more intentionally rather than just driving past their homes when you go somewhere in your car. Take out a piece of paper and draw your street or cul-de-sac. Put the address for each neighbor and their name, along with the names of their children. If you don't know their names, you may need to introduce yourself and say hello.

Help the needy. If you are looking for a neighbor to love, consider the poor, a group that Jesus called His followers to serve.

In a powerful New Testament passage, Jesus describes the final judgment. All of humanity will be divided into two groups: the blessed sheep and the accursed goats. The difference between the sheep and the goats? The sheep carried out Christ's humanitarian mission:

"Come, you who are blessed by my Father; take your inheritance, the kingdom prepared for you since the creation of the world. For I was hungry and you gave me something to eat, I was thirsty and you gave me something to drink, I was a stranger and you invited me in, I needed clothes and you clothed me, I was sick and you looked after me, I was in prison and you came to visit me" (Matthew 25: 35-40).

If you break this passage down, there are six specific ways Jesus is suggesting we reach out to others in need: Food, water, hospitality, clothing, health care, and prison visitation. There are people in your community who desperately need some or all of these things. Could you help some of these people address their needs? If so, you are not only ministering to them but also to Jesus himself.

Jesus described six specific ways his followers would reach out to others in need. Could you help people in your community with some of their needs?

You may not be able to reach out to people in all six of these areas on your own, but you can partner with organizations in your area that do. For example, here in Colorado Springs, Catholic Charities of Central Colorado works to address all six of the needs Christ told us to address in Matthew 25.

This charity depends on more than 100,000 volunteer hours a year, and often needs 50-60 volunteers a day to manage its soup kitchen and other ministries for some of the poorest, most desperate, and most vulnerable members of our community.

The Springs Rescue Mission is another ministry that helps the poor and homeless in our community. There are hundreds of rescue missions around the country that could use your help.

Volunteering with groups like this is ideal for men and women who are trying to serve the poor in retirement. Volunteering uses a valuable resource many retirees have in abundance (time) while conserving their finite resources (finances). When you volunteer to help the poor in your local area, you can serve people who need help, minister to Christ, and impact your community for the better. You might even discover your unique calling.

If you are looking for more meaningful assignments, read through the four Gospels carefully and look for passages that suggest Christian actions you can take.

The Final Challenge: Ending Well

During the 1960s, people started using the term "midlife crisis." Those who experienced such crises might question their identity, doubt their core beliefs, change their careers, or wrestle with self-doubt. Some of them bought sporty red convertibles—or other adult toys—as their marriages crumbled.

Today, people are talking about a new and different crisis. According to geriatric specialists with Johns Hopkins Medicine, many elderly people seem to be experiencing something called a "Later-Life Crisis."

People used to talk about having a midlife crisis. Today, many elderly people seem to be experiencing a "Later-Life Crisis."

If you find yourself spending too much time looking into the rearview mirror, you may be experiencing a midlife, or later-life, crisis," said the Johns Hopkins Medicine article, which suggested a way for dealing with this crisis.

"Reframe what it means to get older. Instead of lamenting what you never did, or what you've lost, (think) about this time as a chance to take on new challenges and embrace life in a new way."

I've seen my share of people experiencing a Later-Life Crisis, and it's not pretty. That's why I encourage people to end well. Continue living a life of purpose until the very end.

I picture life as a big, long race. And if life is a race, we can consider our retirement years the final laps around the track. My hope and prayer is that you may end well by running these final laps with all the gusto and life and intentionality you can muster.

I'm not the first person to see life as a race. The writer of Hebrews shares my hope that people will not to grow weary and lose heart, but remain faithful for a lifetime.

Therefore, since we are surrounded by such a great cloud of witnesses, let us throw off everything that hinders and the sin that so easily entangles. And let us run with perseverance the race marked out for us, fixing our eyes on Jesus, the pioneer and perfecter of faith. For the joy set before him he endured the cross, scorning its shame, and sat down at the right hand of the throne of God. Consider him who endured such opposition from sinners, so that you will not grow weary and lose heart (Hebrews 12:1-3).

Moving Beyond Yourself

When I talk to people about their hopes and dreams for retirement, they often talk about their future in very limited ways: Where they might live. How they might socialize. Where they might go to church.

Reading behind the lines, what I hear many people saying is: "My world is growing smaller and smaller."

Many retirees spend their days in a small condo or apartment, eat or socialize only with the other people in their retiree community, and go out only to visit a doctor or go to the grocery.

All of this is fine, but is something missing? Jesus told his disciples to "go into all the world." But the smaller our dreams, the less impact we will have on the world. Living in a shrinking world puts the focus on us, while Jesus calls us outward to others.

One of the best ways to discover purpose and meaning is to move beyond yourself. Instead of thinking about retirement solely in terms of "me" or "us," start considering this phase of your life as an opportunity to give more attention to "them" and "those."

One of the best ways to discover purpose and meaning is to move beyond yourself.

Who is the "them" you can love and help and serve? That question is yours to answer. But I can promise you that if you enlarge your world, your heart and mind will also grow r in order to accommodate your vision.

Retirement is a wonderful gift. Don't fritter it away. Figure out how to embrace it and use to find your purpose and meaning.

Questions for reflection:

1. What is the value of living with intentionality? Or is there any?
2. Is living with purpose about you? Or, about others?
3. If you don't know where to start in your search for meaning and purpose in this or your next stage of retirement, here are some places to start. Jesus laid out some priorities:
   a. The. Poor
   b. The widows(ers)
   c. The poor in spirit
   d. Those who mourn
   e. Those who hunger
   f. Those who thirst
   g. Those who are sick
   h. Those in jail
   i. The oppressed
   j. Children
   k. Aged
   l. All those in need

All good places to start!

CHAPTER 13

DISCOVERING AND LIVING OUT YOUR CALLING

Mark's gospel describes Jesus as a carpenter (Mark 6:3), while Matthew calls Him "the carpenter's son" (Matthew 13:55). But Bible scholars say it's probably more accurate to call Jesus a "builder," just as people today would describe a jack-of-all-trades who works in the building industry.

Carpentry was probably just one of Jesus' professional skills. Chances are good that He also worked as a stone mason. The region where Jesus grew up had very few trees. Most of the buildings in the region were made of stone, and some of Jesus parables describe how skilled builders lay solid foundations for their projects.

We don't know whether Jesus worked as a day laborer who waited for daily assignments, or whether he was a contract laborer or even a supervisor. Some scholars suggest that anyone involved in the building trades in Jesus' day would have worked on the massive rebuilding project underway at the nearby city of Sephora. Jesus knew how to build, just as a number of his disciples knew how to fish. Building the Kingdom and becoming a fisher of men seem to go together.

The New Testament doesn't tell us much about Jesus' work life, but we do know this: When He was approximately 30 years old, Jesus the builder underwent a professional transition. His life was transformed as He was called to do a new type of work. The timing was an active work of God and reported by John the Baptist.

When Jesus was approximately 30 years old, He underwent a professional transition.

"This is he who was spoken of through the prophet Isaiah," John proclaimed. Then John quoted this relevant portion of Isaiah's prophecy:
A voice of one calling in the wilderness,
'Prepare the way for the Lord ... make straight paths for him' (Matthew 3:2-3).

What's Your Encore?

Author and social entrepreneur Marc Freedman would say Jesus' ministry was His "encore." In his 2007 book, *"Encore: Finding Work that Matters in the Second Half of Life,"* Freedman describes the changes he went through, and the changes others go through when they undergo dramatic vocational transitions in retirement.

Freedman describes a movement of people who celebrate "the freedom to work" in retirement by pursuing a different kind of work than they did before retirement. Freedman says this shift represents a:

... movement of individuals who embody a powerful alternative, who are living out a distinctive and compelling vision of work in the second half of life, one built around the dream of an "encore career" at the intersection of continued income, new meaning, and significance for country and to the greater good.

While Jesus' job transition was inspired by a call from God, Freedman sees a host of factors inspiring professional shifts today:

... longevity, demography, human development, generational experience, fiscal imperatives, labor market dictates, and the particular historical moment combined to lead boomers to contribute longer and to use their education and experience in areas with jobs to offer, deeper meaning to confer, and broader social purposes to fulfill.

Freedman says one of the biggest reasons so many people are seeking encores today is that they reject what modern retirement has become. He describes the changes retirement has undergone:

... stretched from a sensible and justified period of rest and relaxation into a phase as long as midlife in duration, retirement, once a powerful portion of

the American dream, has been distorted into something that no longer works for most individuals — or for the nation.

For me, Jesus is a powerful model of the kinds of "encore careers" Freedman describes, and I'm encouraging everyone I meet to follow His model.

Here's how I describe this transition: For years, you were defined by your work. Now, it's time to turn the tables, redefine your life, and pursue your calling." This may involve work, but it will be a different kind of work than you have known before."

From Purpose to Calling

In the previous chapter, we saw how men and women are combating the meaninglessness of retirement by forging new lives and even careers based on meaning and purpose. You may be curious: What's the difference between purpose and calling?

Purpose is about you, and what makes life meaningful to you.

Calling is about God, and the assignments He has for you to carry out.

Purpose is about you using your wisdom and experience to do something that "fits" your life in retirement.

Calling is about making yourself open and vulnerable so that you can respond fully and obediently to God's leading.

Purpose is about you, and what makes life meaningful to you. Calling is about God, and the assignments He has for you to carry out.

When some people hear the word "calling," they assume it relates to religious work, such as preaching, teaching, pastoring a church, or serving as a missionary. While all of these are respected callings in the church, God does not call everyone to church work. As I've seen in my own case, He calls many of us to serve Him right where we are, doing exactly what we are doing.

By digging into Scripture, we can better understand what calling is all about. For example, the prophet Jeremiah shows that the person who seeks God's calling must be submissive and responsive to His call:

"You, LORD, are our Father.

We are the clay, you are the potter;
we are all the work of your hand" (Jer. 64.8).

Jeremiah describes what calling looks like: You, LORD, are the potter. We are the clay.

In one of His talks with His disciples, Jesus explained that calling originates with Him, not with us: "You did not choose me, but I chose you and appointed you so that you might go and bear fruit—fruit that will last—and so that whatever you ask in my name the Father will give you" (John 15:16).

Jesus described our relationship to Him with an illustration people would have recognized from the vineyards that were so common in the region:

I am the vine; you are the branches. If you remain in me and I in you, you will bear much fruit; apart from me you can do nothing. If you do not remain in me, you are like a branch that is thrown away and withers; such branches are picked up, thrown into the fire and burned. If you remain in me and my words remain in you, ask whatever you wish, and it will be done for you. This is to my Father's glory, that you bear much fruit, showing yourselves to be my disciples (John 15:5-8).

If you are like many people, retirement may be your best opportunity to bear much fruit for God. My passion is to see more men and women in retirement fully embrace this great opportunity to bear fruit for God and bless the world.

"Believer" or "Disciple"?

What does it mean to be a disciple of Jesus? Discipleship means more than merely believing, or going to church, or having the right theology, or memorizing the right Bible verses. It involves doing, growing, and serving others.

The Apostle Paul described this progression in one of his letters:

Therefore, if anyone is in Christ, the new creation has come: The old has gone, the new is here! All this is from God, who reconciled us to himself through Christ and gave us the ministry of reconciliation: that God was reconciling the world to himself in Christ, not counting people's sins against them. And he has committed to us the message of reconciliation. We are therefore Christ's ambassadors, as though God were making his appeal through us. We implore you on Christ's behalf: Be reconciled to God. God made him who had no sin to be sin for us, so that in him we might become the righteousness of God (2 Corinthians 5: 17-21).

Paul explains this progression clearly: Since we have been reconciled to God through Christ, He has now made us His ambassadors in this ministry of reconciliation. In other words, once we have been reconciled to God, our reconciliation does not stop with us, but instead we become reconciler's on God's behalf.

Blessed with Differing Gifts

Each one of us is different and unique, and so are the gifts and calling we have been given. God doesn't create people who are identical copies of each other. Rather, He creates as much diversity in the human family as He does throughout the natural world and the cosmos.

God creates as much diversity in the human family as He does in the natural world and our cosmos.

Paul describes these differences by comparing them to different parts of the human body:

For by the grace given me I say to every one of you: Do not think of yourself more highly than you ought, but rather think of yourself with sober judgment, in accordance with the faith God has distributed to each of you. For just as each of us has one body with many members, and these members do not all have the same function, so in Christ we, though many, form one body, and each member belongs to all the others. We have different gifts, according to the grace given to each of us. If your gift is prophesying, then prophesy in accordance with your faith; if it is serving, then serve; if it is teaching, then teach; if it is to encourage, then give encouragement; if it is giving, then give generously; if it is to lead, do it diligently; if it is to show mercy, do it cheerfully (Romans 12:3-8).

Paul returns to this theme of differing gifts in 1 Corinthians 12:

There are different kinds of gifts, but the same Spirit distributes them.

There are different kinds of service, but the same Lord. There are different kinds of working, but in all of them and in everyone it is the same God at work.

Now to each one the manifestation of the Spirit is given for the common good. To one there is given through the Spirit a message of wisdom, to another a message of knowledge by means of the same Spirit, to another faith by the same Spirit, to another gifts of healing by that one Spirit, to another miraculous powers, to another prophecy, to another distinguishing between spirits, to another speaking in different kinds of tongues, and to still another the interpretation of tongues. All these are the work of one and the same Spirit, and he distributes them to each one, just as he determines (1 Corinthians 12:4-11).

God has gifted you, and there is work He would like you to do to exercise those gifts.

Navigating the River of Life

People often talk about "finding their calling," as if a calling is something that is hidden somewhere awaiting their discovery. I believe it's more accurate to talk about how our calling *finds us.*

As I see the process playing out in my own life and the lives of others, it seems that a calling is not something that suddenly lands in our laps, fully formed and gift-wrapped. Rather, our calling is revealed to us gradually as we navigate the river of life.

A few years back, Judy and I were vacationing with another couple along the Battenkill River in Vermont. The name may be less than inviting, but the river itself is beautiful.

One afternoon, I took my leave from the other three members of our group to pursue one of my lifelong passions: canoeing. For the next two or three hours, I was going with the flow. The experience was both peaceful and exhilarating. It seemed that in every way the river was just right: not too big, not too slow, and not offering too many rapids to navigate.

At one point during the afternoon, I remember lying back, relaxing, then looking up at the sky. Before I knew it, I was praising God.

"Thank you, God, for creating this beautiful river, and for giving me the ability to enjoy this portion of your creation so thoroughly."

Right at that moment, I felt I was in the middle of God's will. By that I don't mean to suggest that God was calling me to quit my job and to spend my life canoeing. It was something deeper. I was experiencing joy by doing something He created for me to enjoy.

I was experiencing joy by enjoying something He created for me to enjoy.

As I gently flowed down the Battenkill that day, I was feeling like Olympic runner Eric Liddell. I remember his powerful line of dialogue from the movie, "Chariots of Fire." Liddell said, "I believe God made me for a purpose, but he also made me fast. And when I run, I feel his pleasure."

When I canoe, I feel God's pleasure. My own life experience played a role in my pleasure that afternoon. For example, I used to teach canoeing to young people at a summer camp in Wisconsin. This experience is part of what makes my joys different from those of others. Judy doesn't derive as much joy from canoeing as I do, but I've sought out great canoeing rivers in Costa Rica and Wales.

Over the years I have canoed on many rivers around the world and I've developed a deep knowledge of how to navigate them and avoid all the mishaps. For me, gliding down these ribbons of water brings the same kind of joy that others get from appreciating great works of art or rereading some of their favorite books.

I believe God uses joy to help us find our calling. God created you, and He wired you in particular ways. He placed you in space and time, knowing the powerful experiences you would have. Now He wants to use all of this for his glory and the building of His eternal Kingdom.

God is calling you to use your gifts and experiences for something bigger than yourself. If you want to respond to His call, keep your eyes open for opportunities that have these four essential ingredients:

1) Your unique preparation.

You are unique, and no one else has enjoyed the experiences and learning opportunities you have. If you speak Chinese or Arabic, perhaps Christ would like you to use your unique gifts to carry out the Great Commission he assigned to *all* of his disciples, including us:

All authority in heaven and on earth has been given to me. Therefore, go and make disciples of all nations, baptizing them in the name of the Father and of the Son and of the Holy Spirit, and teaching them to obey everything I have commanded you. And surely, I am with you always, to the very end of the age (Matthew 28:18-20).

Your Chinese or Arabic language skills could help you accomplish the three specific tasks Christ mentioned: Making disciples, baptizing people, and teaching them.

You may have other skills that are desperately needed. Ministries of every kind need people with expertise in accounting, personnel, technology, communications, and marketing. Would you be willing to use your experience and preparation to serve God, either across the world or in your own town?

Would you be willing to use your experience and preparation to serve God, either across the world or in your own town?

Think of all the complex challenges you have learned to face, the detailed tasks you have managed to tackle, the specialized skills you have gained, and the connections you have made. Don't walk away from all of these wonderful gifts when you retire, but instead find ways to put your unique preparation to work in making the world a better place.

2) Your natural gifts.

One person is an introvert while another is an extrovert. One tendency is not necessarily better than the other, but the extrovert may function better in public, while the introvert works better on his own.

One person is a generalist who can tackle anything that comes her way, while the other is a specialist who is an expert in her field. Both skill sets are valuable, but they're are not the same and lead to different kinds of work and productivity.

There are many varieties of natural gifts. Some people can remember long strings of numbers, while others have finely honed tonal discrimination and can immediately tell the difference between one musical note and another. Some people are good at juggling complex intellectual concepts, while others are skilled at immediately determining the spatial relationships between various objects.

During our working years, most of us carved out careers that used some of our natural gifts, but left others underutilized. Now is your chance to find out where you excel and to put your abilities to work in a way that fulfills your calling.

Now is your chance to find out where you excel and put those abilities to work in a way that fulfills your calling.

3) Your spiritual gifts

The apostle Paul's New Testament letters repeatedly emphasize the importance of spiritual gifts in the life of believers and the work of church. Some people assume that spiritual gifts are restricted to the five offices or roles that Paul lays out in Ephesians 4:

- Apostle
- Prophet
- Evangelist
- Pastor
- Teacher.

But elsewhere, Paul makes it clear that Gods spiritual gifts are for all believers, not just pastors and other prominent leaders. In his letter to the Romans, Paul challenges Christian believers to invest themselves in the life of the Church, listing some of the key spiritual gifts we can use to build up the body:

For just as each of us has one body with many members, and these members do not all have the same function, so in Christ we, though many, form one body, and each member belongs to all the others. We have different gifts, according to the grace given to each of us. If your gift is prophesying, then prophesy in accordance with your faith; if it is serving, then serve; if it is teaching, then teach; if it is to encourage, then give encouragement; if it is giving, then give generously; if it is to lead, do it diligently; if it is to show mercy, do it cheerfully (Romans 12:4-8).

Here Paul lists six additional spiritual gifts:

- Prophecy
- Service
- Teaching
- Encouragement
- Giving
- Showing mercy.

Are you blessed with any of the gifts Paul lists here? If so, seek to use these gifts for God's glory. If not, check out the slightly different list of gifts that Paul describes in 1 Corinthians 12:

- Word of wisdom
- Word of knowledge
- Faith
- Gifts of healing
- Miracles
- Distinguishing between spirits
- Tongues
- Interpretation of tongues
- Helps
- Administration.

Do you have any of the spiritual gifts on these lists? As Spirit filled Christians, we all have spiritual gifts. If so, God wants you to offer them to the church to build up the Body of Christ. Don't be merely a pew sitter. Be a member-in-full who invests your spiritual gifts into the life of the church.

4) Your opportunities to work and serve

Bob and Bill were brothers, and both were raised in the church. But when Bill went to college, he gradually lost his faith in Christ and increasingly referred to himself as "spiritual." For Bob, who remained a passionate believer, Bill's pilgrimage away from faith was deeply troubling. Now, years later, Bob has developed a unique spiritual gift. He will spend hours talking to troubled college students about their intellectual problems with the Christian faith.

After growing up in a troubled home with an alcoholic father, Nancy thought she had found the perfect partner in Charles. But 10 years into their marriage, Charles became addicted to gambling (both in Las Vegas and online). He gradually used up the family's savings before walking away from them without saying goodbye. Nancy's broken relationships with the two addicted men in her life have given her a deep compassion for people who struggle with addiction. She volunteers at her church, hosting meetings for two groups that serve people with similar struggles: Alcoholics Anonymous and Celebrate Recovery.

What moves you?
What's your passion?
What wrong must you right?
What cause must you take up?
Who do you want to help, and how?
How have your life experiences shaped who you are and what you can do?
What's your calling?

Poet, writer, and Presbyterian minister Frederick Buechner has been one of the most quotable Christian writers since C. S. Lewis. His insightful description shows him at his most quotable: "The place God calls you to is the place where your deep gladness and the world's deep hunger meet."

Rethinking Retirement

Once upon a time, you may have pictured retirement as a period of rest, relaxation, and recreation. After all, you worked for many years, and you wanted to spend your retirement years doing something other than working.

But God offers you wonderful and urgently needed opportunities to use your gifts in service to Him and the world.

"Always give yourselves fully to the work of the Lord, because you know that your labor in the Lord is not in vain," said Paul in 1 Corinthians 15:58.

This work can be hard, but the rewards are meaningful, and the returns from your investment will last into eternity.

The one reward I look forward to the most is the one Jesus told His disciples about in one of his parables. A man is going away, so he entrusts his possessions to his servants. Later, he rewarded those who invested those possessions and made them grow.

"Well done, good and faithful servant! You have been faithful with a few things; I will put you in charge of many things. Come and share your master's happiness!" (Matthew 25: 23).

Questions for Reflection:

1. Do you need to discover your calling, or take next steps to carry it out?
2. What does it mean to you to, "live out your calling?"
3. Who do you know who personifies this for you? Describe the person or couple:
4. At the very end of your life, what would you like to hear?
5. What are your next steps to being Faithful for a Lifetime?

CHAPTER 14

EMBRACING YOUR MINISTRY

When I was a younger businessman, I saw him nearly every morning as I stopped for breakfast or a meeting at Coco's Bakery Restaurant on Lake Avenue in Pasadena. There were two things that immediately stood out to me.

One was the age differences. The man seemed to be in his 60s or 70s, but the various men he met with seemed to be in their 20s.

The other was the length and depth of the conversations he had. It was not uncommon for him to spend two or more hours involved in intensive back-and-forth discussions.

Only later would I learn his name and a few more things about him. He was Evon Hedley. He was an executive who worked for World Vision in California after years serving Youth for Christ in Illinois. Over the years he held different positions for a variety of Christian ministries. But no matter what he did for work, one of his favorite ministries was keeping a busy schedule of mentoring meetings with young men.

"I always thought of my mentoring session not as a Bible study or a prayer meeting but rather application of the Bible," he said in an article about him on the website of Pasadena's Lake Avenue Church, where he worshipped and served for more than 50 years.

"I like to encourage them and see where they are, helping them in areas where they need help. We would find a passage to help solve it as well as pray. Most times I have met the guys over a meal or in the car."

I recently learned that Evon died in 2018 at the age of 102. He had continued his ministry of mentoring well into his 90s.

Evon Hedley is a wonderful role model for men and women who seek to minister to others during retirement. Although he was a talented executive and fundraiser for large, influential ministries, he loved nothing more than sitting down with people one-on-one.

What about you? Do you desire to minister to others? Do you sense God calling you to minister in particular ways? If so, get ready to experience one of the most exciting and invigorating activities you can do in retirement: Serving God and loving your neighbor.

All Are Ministers

Christianity is not a spectator sport. Those who are redeemed are also called to work as redeemers. *Everyone* is called to minister, no matter your age, gender, profession, or educational level.

For years there was a big banner on the auditorium wall of Lake Avenue Church. The banner read, "We are all ministers together." I saw that banner every Sunday for years, and I think it finally sunk in!

Everyone is called to minister, no matter your age, gender, profession, or educational level.

That doesn't mean everyone is called to *be a minister*. The office of pastor is a special calling. And it doesn't mean you need to be ordained as a priest, pastor, or minister even though Christians believe in a concept called "the priesthood of all believers."

Martin Luther, who was a Catholic priest before he underwent a personal transformation and launched the Protestant Reformation, once wrote, "This word priest should become as common as the word Christian" because all believers are priests. All believers have a direct relationship with God."

Luther wrote these words in his commentary on the New Testament epistles of Peter and Jude. Peter showed how ministry was something everyone should do in this powerful passage:

"Come to Jesus Christ. He is the living stone that people have rejected, but which God has chosen and highly honored. And now you are living stones that are being used to build a spiritual house. You are also a group of holy priests, and with the help of Jesus Christ you will offer sacrifices that please God (1 Peter 2:4-5).

Perhaps you've never thought of yourself as being part of "a group of holy priests." But it's time you start thinking that way.

"God says that you are a priest," writes Saddleback Church founder Rick Warren.

"Depending on your background, that may be scary or confusing."

Many Christians have embraced a flawed, "professionalized" view of ministry that says there are leaders (usually pastors of churches), and there are followers (all the members of churches). The job of pastors is to minister, they say, and the job of believers is to be ministered to. But Warren and many other leaders reject this simplistic dichotomy. All Christians are ministers and should be doing the work of ministry.

"How do you know what your ministry is?" asks Warren. "Look at your talents, gifts, and abilities. When you use those talents and gifts to help other people, that's called ministry — nothing fancy or scary about it. It's just helping others."

This is not esoteric theory but life-changing reality. You have a ministry. That may not necessarily mean your work will take place in a church or religious organization, but it may. Let's take a look at some of the many ministry opportunities that are waiting for ministers.

A World of Opportunities both Near and Far

There is much in the world that needs to be done.

There is much you can do.

Your goal is to find your ministry at the intersection of your capability and the world's need. Your opportunities are limitless, both in your back yard and around the globe.

When people start exploring their ministry opportunities, they often ask these questions as they try to ascertain what they should do and where they should do it.

Find your ministry at the intersection of your capability and the world's need.

Should I serve in a church, or some other Christian organization?

Or should I serve in a group that has no religious affiliation?

Should I serve in missions, following Bruce to Timbuktu, or some equally remote corner of the globe?

Or should I roll up my sleeves right here in my own home town?

My answers to this question are: Yes. Yes. Yes. And yes. All of these forms of service are needed and valuable.

Keep your eyes on that intersection between of the world's need and your capabilities while we review some of the primary avenues for finding and doing your ministry.

Plentiful Opportunities Nearby

You don't need to travel to Timbuktu in order to fulfill your ministry in retirement. In fact, you can have a greater positive impact on people you may already know and love through grandparenting, mentoring, and coaching.

Retirement opens new opportunities for loving your grandchildren, and there are ministries and organizations that can help you be an even better grandparent.

"Grandparents play a unique and profoundly influential role in the lives of grandchildren—second only to parents," say the leaders of a group called the Legacy Coalition. "Today's grandparents don't consider themselves to be "seniors" in the traditional sense. They are generally healthier and more vital than any other generation of grandparents in history."

The Coalition offers training seminars and an annual convention that "equip and encourage this generation of active grandparents to stay connected and involved with their grandchildren in positive and powerful ways."

Grandchildren aren't the only people you can serve in retirement. Like Evon Hedley in our opening story, you can be a mentor or coach to people who are younger than you and can grow from your wisdom.

So, what is a mentor? Dictionaries define it as an experienced and trusted advisor.

So, how does a mentor find mentees? If there's a young person you know from church or work that you think you could help, invite them out for a coffee or lunch. Ask them about their lives and listen to what they say. If the other person wants you to be a mentor, it will become clear as you talk. You can also see if youth ministers who work with teens or college students know of young people you could mentor. The critical variable is your availability.

Coaching is similar but often more formal and more focused. In the business world, many people seek out and hire coaches who can help them with leadership and other skills. There are many specialized forms of coaching, so you can find one that fits your skills and experience.

SCORE is one great example of a volunteer organization that provides free business advice to entrepreneurs and small business people. With 300 offices around the company, SCORE is a great way to offer guidance and insight to the next generation of business leaders.

Think about your own life and the help you received along the way from grandparents, mentors, or coaches. Wouldn't you like to pass it on by coming alongside another person and helping them navigate the challenges of life?

The Retirement Reformation believes mentoring and coaching are critical. Opportunities for both are available through the website. www. RetirementReformation.org.

Serving the local church.

There are hundreds of thousands of churches in America, from 10,000-member megachurches to storefront gatherings with a few dozen souls. Local congregations in the body of Christ depend on their members to keep things functioning. For retirees, serving churches offers limitless opportunities.

But many churches give their older members the following mixed messages:

- Don't stop your financial giving.

- Don't be grumpy, and while you're at it, try not to fulfill young people's other "codger" images by turning up your nose at rock-style worship music.
- As for what you can do in a positive sense, we're not sure. Maybe you can be a greeter or usher, take up the offering, help out in with the kids in the nursery, set up chairs and tables for congregational events, and clean up afterwards.

Unfortunately, these churches are missing a golden opportunity to enlist caring, capable workers. It may be up to you to educate church leaders about the benefits you and other seniors can bring to the congregation. A recent post on Thom Rainer's "Growing Healthy Churches" blog provided some proactive steps you can take:

1) Ask me to serve. Sometimes it easy for me to think I'm not as needed as I used to be. I realize the church needs younger leadership at some point, and I don't want to get in the way of that transition. I'll help in any way I can, but you may need to recruit me directly.

2) Trust me with some of your prayer concerns. Some of us have spent decades trying to figure out how to pray, and many of us have more time than others to pray. I want to pray specifically and intentionally for you as my spiritual leaders. Share a bit of your heart with me, and I'll be on board with you.

3) Invite me to join you on a ministry visit. I know that would take more of your time, but I'd be genuinely honored to assist you. If I can, I'll even clear my calendar to help you. I've been around long enough to know not to take your invitation lightly.

4) If you're a church planter, recruit me. I'd want you to talk to my pastor also, but you might find that I'm praying about and looking for a new adventure. The older I get, the more I want to make sure I'm maximizing my gifts for the kingdom. I can tell you for certain that I'll be your friend if we're walking together for God's glory.

There are many ways you can serve in the church, but it may be up to you to overcome some of ageist barriers as you seem to fulfill your calling.

Serving Mission Organizations

Christians have been on a mission to reach people for Christ ever since Jesus commissioned his disciples to "go to all the world." Today, nearly half a million Americans are serving as missionaries around the world, and increasing numbers of them are seniors, thanks to mission agencies and networks that intentionally seek out older workers. A brief Google search reveals a world of opportunities.

Today, nearly half a million Americans are serving as missionaries around the world. Increasing numbers of them are seniors

"You're never too old to be involved in missions," says a headline on the website of Baptist World Mission. "Unfortunately, the idea of 'over the hill' seems to have affected many seniors in what they feel they think they can do for the Lord. Dedicated Christians with early retirement packages could go to a mission field and not have to raise financial support through deputation."

Mission NeXT, a ministry that helps connect people with missionary positions, lists opportunities for various age groups, including those who are 60 and over:

"Do you feel it? It's God's tug. You know because you've been following it for years, and He is faithful. As your schedule opens up, you're searching for fresh purpose and useful opportunities. You are exploring ways to contribute, *but what way is right for you?*"

United World Mission features a testimony from a missionary named Jeff:

"I was a mechanical engineer and my wife was an elementary school teacher. At the time we had mountainous debt and no theological training. Over the next seven years we eliminated our debt, studied the Bible for a year, found a mission agency, raised full support and then left for the desert of Northwest Kenya. We have never been sorry, and we have never thought we were too old.

"God led us to a mission agency which believes that 'second-career' missionaries bring valuable maturity and life experience to missions that is not available from younger graduates. In recent years, more agencies have begun to appreciate these same values."

Ronald was nearing retirement when he made a switch and served in Ethiopia with the organization Hope in View:

"I was over 60 when I first went overseas for an extended time," Ronald said, "but the past 12 years have been among the most fruitful in my life. The big asset we older people have is life experience. If you're in good health, you're never too old."

Missionaries serve in a variety of positions and places, from remote rural outposts and in megacities of 10 million people or more. Some missionaries build and lead churches, while others focus on raising up and training indigenous leaders in their own countries.

I have talked to many successful businessmen and women who tell me they regret doing "secular" work and wish they had instead become a missionary when they were young. But there's no need for regret. Growing numbers of mission agencies are intentionally seeking out older people with string business backgrounds.

"What if the untapped business resources in the church globally were released for missional impact?" asks the website for Business as Mission, a network that has helped many make the transition from business to mission. "We want business men and women to understand God's redemptive work through business in the world. We want to help change the message that Christian business people are hearing and mobilize them for action."

Once upon a time, mission organizations intentionally recruited young missionaries, believing only they could withstand the many pressures and challenges Christian workers can face. But it's a new world now, and more agencies are realizing that there are golden opportunities for people in their golden years.

Serving Other Ministries

In many nations, churches and denominations exert the greatest influence in believers' lives, but in post-World War II America, parachurch groups— the tens of thousands of nonprofit organizations such as Compassion International and Fellowship of Christian Athletes—often have a greater influence than churches.

"Para" comes from the Greek word "alongside," and parachurch organizations are intended to work alongside or assist the church, much like a paramedic works with a doctor. Unlike churches, which employ ordained clergy, adhere to well-defined doctrines, and serve broad-based memberships, parachurch organizations are nonprofit corporations which are typically led and staffed by lay people. They often focus on a particular set of issues or needs, such as Bible translation and distribution, family values, or relief and development.

Parachurch organizations' reliance on lay leaders and employees has unleashed a flood of talent into the world. And their ecumenical spirit often allows them to transcend narrow denominational distinctives, a fact that has led some observers to conclude that parachurch organizations, not churches, best illustrate the universality of the body of Christ.

There are parachurch organizations serving men, women, teens, and children. There are groups that work with athletes (from rodeo cowboys and cowgirls to bow hunters), ex-prisoners, long-haul truckers, recovering prostitutes and the disabled. If you have a passion to serve a particular group of people, there are probably parachurch organizations that are working to meet that need.

Local Charities and Social Service Organizations

Fifteen percent of Americans live in poverty.

More than 20 million Americans struggle with alcohol or drug abuse.

Some 40 million Americans are largely illiterate, able only to understand the simplest written instructions.

One in eight Americans struggles to find enough to eat every day.

More than half a million Americans are homeless.

Right now, people struggle with these and other problems in your community. And right now, there are people just like you working to help those who struggle. Would you like to roll up your sleeves and get involved in helping people who need help the most? If so, there are plenty of opportunities to make a big difference in the lives of people who live next door or across town.

In previous chapters we mentioned Catholic charities and rescue missions, and these groups operate in hundreds of cities around the U.S.

There are also thousands of smaller, local charities founded to address specific local needs.

Do your homework and you can find out what needs your community has and which organizations are doing something to help.

Funding Your Future Ministry

Your financial planning for retirement will impact what kind of ministry you can do. If you have saved enough for retirement, you can offer your services to a wide range of ministries, some of which do not pay well or at all.

But if you still need to generate income during retirement, you will need to work for a congregation or organization that can offer a decent salary and benefits. How about part time work for pay with a purpose, and the other half for no pay and a purpose?

A Ministry Just for You

The "Help Wanted" signs are everywhere. Ministries and organizations need what you have. There's nobody quite like you in the world, and I look forward to seeing the unique ministry opportunity that you embrace.

Please note that the Retirement Reformation will be affiliating with churches and other ministries who embrace the idea of purposeful retirement and are putting meaningful opportunities in place for members or other supporters. Look for the symbol of Retirement Reformation affiliates.

R E T I R E M E N T
Reformation

FREEDOM WITH FAITH...FOR A LIFETIME

Question for reflection:

1. What is your definition of ministry?
2. How will you embrace it?
3. How do you think it will change from one Life-stage to another?
4. Detail how the Retirement Reformation message changed or informed your thinking?
5. How has the Retirement Reformation message changed what you will do? What next steps you will take?
6. Are you ready to take next steps in your Retirement Reformation journey?

CHAPTER 15

THE RETIREMENT REFORMATION: TRANSFORMING HOW WE LIVE OUT THE LAST DECADES OF OUR LIVES

Dave and I spotted each other from opposite sides of the sanctuary one Sunday morning, and we caught up with each other out in the atrium after the service. We hadn't talked to each other in months because he had been traveling for work, and when he wasn't traveling it seemed I was traveling.

We agreed to meet the following week for breakfast. I didn't have any agenda or expectations for our time together, but after Dave sat down and we quickly caught up on all our activities, I could tell there was something on his mind.

"What is it?" I asked.

"I guess the simplest way to explain it is to say that I think you have totally ruined my upcoming retirement." There was a hint of a smile on his face.

I was momentarily taken aback.

"What you mean?" I asked, not quite sure what Dave meant.

"Well, it's pretty simple. Six months ago, before you and I started talking, I thought I knew what retirement was all about. It was simple.

You work, you save, and then you retire and work on your bucket list until you spend all your money, and then you die."

"So, where would you say you stand on retirement today?"

"That's the thing. I really don't know anymore. I used to think I knew what retirement was all about, but then you came along and upset my applecart. Now, I'm not so sure. I'm trying to figure out if there's a different approach I can take toward retirement, but I don't really know what it is yet."

That was the moment I saw that some of my ideas about a better way to understand retirement were getting through to Dave. He was digging down and questioning his own ideas about retirement. He was finding he didn't buy into our culture's prevailing assumptions about the final decades of life. He was having an aha moment and seemed ready to make major changes in the way he was hoping to live the rest of his life.

Some of my missionary friends might call Dave a "convert." I've worked with missionaries for decades. Some of them serve in countries that are hostile to Christianity, and I've heard more than a few express their frustration at never being sure they had brought any nonbelievers to faith in Christ.

I knew Dave's change of heart about retirement was a big deal, so I responded by letting him know about a project I've been working on in secret for years.

"I'm not trying to create a First Church of Bruce, but I do have a dream. My dream is to serve God by launching a movement that I call the Retirement Reformation."

"What in the world is that?" asked Dave.

"I'm so glad you asked!"

Seeking a New Model

It had been months since Dave and I met for breakfasts and lunches. When Dave and his wife Terri attended the talks on "Reframing Retirement" I gave at a local church, I saw Dave furiously scribbling notes. But we hadn't talked to each other since then, and I didn't know if anything had impacted him. After catching up, I asked him to explain.

"So, what exactly have I done to ruin retirement for you? Tell me what you meant by that."

"Well, now that I see how long I may be retired, I want to do something meaningful with all that time."

"OK, let's take it step-by-step," said. "Lay it all out for me?"

"Well, the first thing that struck me is how long retirement lasts these days. I grew up seeing retirement is something that lasted five or ten or maybe fifteen years, not two or three decades. So that's one thing I need to reevaluate."

"That's good," I said. "Not everybody goes through that process of recalibrating longevity."

"One thing's for sure, I don't want to spend that much of my life doing nothing. At first, I didn't see why you kept talking about 'nothing.' Now I want to make sure that's not how I spend retirement.

"And when we talked about Sun City and looked at those ads for retirement communities, that part of it began bugging me, too. My dad lived his last years in a very nice, very expensive retirement community. But he never really enjoyed life there, and just seemed to draw into himself more. His final inward step was to kind of give up and die."

"It depends, doesn't it?" I asked. "My parents were perfectly happy living in Sun City, but when I visited them, I could tell that not everyone there was equally happy with that kind of lifestyle."

"Exactly. But probably the biggest thing you ruined for me was my idea that retirement is a time to finally kick back, relax, and enjoy all the parts of life I wasn't been able to enjoy before. But now I wonder if kicking back will give me any purpose or meaning. I guess I realize I've embraced a secular approach that says you work and then you retire, and once you retire, the goal is jamming as much leisure as you can into the remaining time you have. And then you die"

Dave turned to some comments he had written in his notebook.

"I'm trying to connect my ideas about retirement to deeper things in life, like my faith in Christ. But instead of asking, What Would Jesus Do? my question is more like," How would Jesus retire?"

I thought about that for a moment. HWJR? It doesn't roll off the tongue like WWJD, but it might work!

"I guess I have problems picturing Jesus spending decades of his life just playing shuffleboard, or whatever recreational activities they had back in Jesus' day."

"I never thought about Jesus playing shuffleboard before, but I think I agree with you. I could see Jesus playing some shuffleboard, but it probably wouldn't be the focus of His life."

"The focus of my life has been work," Dave said. "My time with Terri, my time for personal interests, my time for church and personal spiritual growth has been squeezed by everything else I'm required to do. I don't want God to get squeezed in retirement. I want spiritual priorities to take a bigger place for once."

Dave didn't realize it, but he's the perfect person to join the Retirement Reformation, an emerging movement of people who want to live retirement with meaning and purpose.

A Brief History of Movements

So, what makes up a movement, anyway? And how is a movement different from an organization, a company, or even an idea?

From Martin Luther's Protestant Reformation to the Civil Rights movement of Martin Luther King, Jr., mass social movements typically arise when people experience the following four essential elements:

- A common problem that is experienced by many people and easily observed by others.
- A common lexicon describing the problem and exploring possible solutions.
- A common connection for movement activists to communicate, interact, and organize.
- And a common agreement about the best solutions to the problem, along with action steps that people can take to make a change for the better.

One example of such a movement is the revolution that led to the creation of the United States of America. All four of the essential elements were there.

- The common problem was the New World colonists' growing anger over unjust taxes levied by England on everything from paper, to glass, to tea.
- The common lexicon was found in freedom-loving slogans, including "No taxation without representation!" and "Don't tread on me," which pictured the colonies as a coiled snake ready to strike at British rule.
- The common means of connection for colonist activists included the public square, local taverns and pubs, and the colonies' growing number of local newspapers published by Benjamin Franklin and others.
- Colonists decided that resistance to British rule was the only solution to their problems. A group called the Sons of Liberty, which included Patrick Henry and Paul Revere, kicked things off with a newsworthy public demonstration: the Boston Tea Party. More than 300 large chests of British tea were broken open and thrown into Boston Harbor. Soon there would be additional "tea parties" in Boston and in states including Maryland, New York, and South Carolina.

There would be no United States without the popular movement that rose to resist—and ultimately rebel against—British rule. These pioneering statesmen redefined freedom in their time, and the Constitution they wrote still inspires and guides us today.

Movements have been major factors in social change for millennia. Remember how Moses led some 1,000,000 Israelites out slavery during the Exodus? Remember how Mahatma Gandhi used non-violent resistance to help India achieve independence from Great Britain? Remember movements for women's rights, temperance, the abolition of slavery, and the environment?

More recently, do you remember how "MeToo" changed the national debate about the sexual abuse of women? Or how Black Lives Matter focused attention on the issues of race and law enforcement? Or how Donald Trump's plan to "Make America Great Again" rewrote America's political playbook? Or how a resistance movement arose to push back against the President?

An influential movement can change the world, and that's part of why being part of a movement is so thrilling. It's exciting to join with many different people who are unified by their passion, connected through their activist, and working together to seek a better and more just tomorrow.

Movements also change people, and they provide a place where people can walk alongside other men and women who are seeking better ways to live. Movements can help people like Dave, who are desperately seeking better ways to retire.

In many ways, my vision for people like Dave mirror's Paul's vision for the church:

… speaking the truth in love, we will grow to become in every respect the mature body of him who is the head, that is, Christ. [16] From him the whole body, joined and held together by every supporting ligament, grows and builds itself up in love, as each part does its work (Ephesians 4:15-16).

Your Invitation to Join the Retirement Reformation

I told Dave all about the Retirement Reformation movement, explaining how the movement shares some of Dave's main concerns about America's broken retirement models, and seeks ways to live the last decades of life with meaning and purpose.

I gave Dave a personal invitation to join up, and I'm making the same offer to you, dear reader. I formally invite you to join The Retirement Reformation. Here's our manifesto:

The Retirement Reformation Manifesto

The Retirement Reformation is committed to encouraging a movement where every Christ follower is confident in God's plan for a lifetime of faithful service and committed to helping the Body of Christ reform its understanding of retirement, then bearing fruit without measure. We assert the biblical truth that Jesus followers are called to bear fruit in every season of life and affirm that commitment with these 10 principles:

1. *Freedom: We live for more than our culture's definition and expectations of retirement. Reforming retirement requires a reframing of our thinking, allowing us to shine a light into the purposeless retirement void and finding freedom from unending leisure, indulgence, and self-gratification.*

2. *Preparation: We choose to enter each new season with a God-directed vision of His preferred future for us. Every season of life prepares us for the next. Each of us needs encouragement, training, equipping and coaching as we seek to live out a lifetime of faithful service.*

3. *Contentment: We embrace the promise of the fruits of the Spirit and reject the self-indulgent trappings of retirement. Our vision of a lifetime of service requires re-focusing, re-positioning, re-vamping, and re-energizing as we prepare for, enter, or experience retirement. The allure of doing "nothing" with eternal value, fades quickly.*

4. *Stewardship: We realize retirement may extend for thirty years or longer. The reality of longevity demands that we see all retirement seasons as a resource to be appreciated, embrace, valued and to faithfully steward. We are committed to healthy living.*

5. *Love: We acknowledge that people matter to God and we cultivate our hearts for others. As we grow closer to God, He will give us the capacity and opportunity to revitalize valued relationships and have great kingdom impact on those He puts in our path.*

6. *Community: We need community and connection with others in authentic relationship. Our retirement years are best spent in community. It is in community with family, friends, fellow believers, plus the weak, poor and disenfranchised where we both learn and serve. The intergenerational church provides community between and among believers.*

7. *Intentionality: We recognize that Our calling ends at death, not retirement. Our entire lives are designed for a purpose. We can continue to grow spiritually and emotionally. This allows God to redeem our past mistakes, revitalize broken relationships and strengthen our commitment to our unique calling. We will follow His purpose, bear fruit, and experience the joy of being a disciple of Jesus.*

8. *Focus: We intentionally focus our activities on Kingdom building activities. Not every activity is beneficial especially those that are*

only self-indulgent. Our priority are those activities growing God's Kingdom; Those activities will lead to the expansion of His Church. We need Jesus and His Holy Spirit to commission and guide our activities.

9. *Service: We live on mission for Jesus, representing him to others. God calls each of us to be on mission during every stage of life. An important role for those in retirement is to pass on wisdom learned and encourage the next generation. Coaching, mentoring, volunteering and grandparenting are valuable opportunities available to us.*

10. *Advocacy: We resolve to encourage others to find meaning and purpose following God's design. Our conviction leads us to shine God's light on each of our paths, pointing to lives filled with meaning and purpose. Our passion and convictions lead us to encourage all to live lives filled with meaning and purpose. Each of us, including all Pastors, ministry leaders and Jesus follows are called to this Retirement Reformation. A new opportunity exists to change the world for Jesus, bear fruit in His name, and experience the abundant life in Him.*

We recognize that it is the power of Jesus that allows us to live with faith and experience fulfillment in every season of life. With that conviction we embrace John 15:16 as our foundation:

"You did not choose me, but I chose you and called you so that you might bear fruit – fruit that will last – and whatever you ask in My Father's name, He will give it to you."

[See www.RetirementReformation.org for the full version and shortened version, both can be printed out for your reference.]

"So, What's Next?"

I watched as Dave quickly read through the manifesto, and after he reached the bottom of the document, he looked up at me.

"This is awesome. I think I agree with everything in here. Where do I sign up? And what do I do next?"

"It tells you right there," I said, pointing to the fourth clause in the manifesto.

"This movement is about thinking, being, and doing things differently than we have before. So, let's think about what you can do to transform your life in those three areas."

Suddenly Dave opened up a big notebook and started taking notes. It was the same notebook he used when he came to the talks on retirement I gave at church.

"Let's start with your ***thinking***. You are asking some great questions, and you can see the holes in some of America's major beliefs about retirement. But I don't think you are done with the thinking stage yet.

"Dave, the wonderful thing about your situation is that you haven't retired yet. What a gift. Since I helped ruin your old ideas about retirement, let me suggest a few resources that can really help you transform your thinking. There are some amazing thought leaders who are doing some great work in this space and connecting the dots between our deepest values and what we are going to do with the rest of our lives. I recommend you check out some of their books. A partial list is available at www. RetirementReformation.org

"Great," Dave said. "I didn't realize thinkers like this were out there. You hear so many voices talking about retirement that it gets confusing."

"OK. The transformation of your thinking is well underway. Let's talk about ***being*** now. We want to see a transformation in your doing, in the way you live. Is there anything you've done, any action or behavior you take, that reflects some of the thinking you've been doing since your old ideas of retirement fell apart?"

Dave thought for a moment.

"There is one thing, a small thing. You could say I'm being more intentional. When you gave me those assignments to write down my Top Ten Retirement Goals, I started a file. And pretty much every weekend, usually on Sunday afternoon, I open that file, take a look at what I've written before, and try to add a few more thoughts. I'm trying to get clearer about what kind of person I really want to be in retirement."

"Congratulations. That may be seem like a small thing, but it's significant. Any work you do on that list today will pay off for years down the road. OK, that's the short summary of transformed being. On to ***doing***.

"It will be interesting to see how the goals you are spelling out on that list impact all the decisions you will be making as you approach retirement. That's what transformed doing is all about."

Answer the Call: Join the Retirement Reformation Movement

There's a movement taking shape across America as men and women question the old assumptions about retirement and devise new ways to experience joy and fulfillment in their post-work years.

Will you join us? Are you ready to be part of a growing community of believers who seek nothing less than the reformation of our ideas about retirement? And the actions steps that follow.

A Seven Step Action Plan

1) Review

Go back and closely examine some of the key lessons in this book. Underline and annotate passages as you do your review. Make your own list of the key ideas and issues that speak to you. Highlight the action steps that go with your new understanding.

2) Reflect

Consider everything we have explored in the previous pages. Which lessons speak to you most directly? What have you learned? How have your ideas changed? Pray through your new understandings.

Which lessons offer solutions to people you know and love? What points are worth discussing with your partner or other family members? Which suggestions can help friends or? coworkers you know who are struggling with retirement issues?

3) Seek

Take these lessons about meaning and purpose in the last third of life to God in prayer. Seek

God's guidance for how you can use your lifetime to bear much fruit (John 15:16), fruit that will last.

4) Join us

Visit the Retirement Reformation website and sign our manifesto [link]. Stand with many others who share your passion for and commitment to reforming retirement in our time?

5) Pass it on

Are there people you know who could benefit from knowing about the issues we have explored in this book?

Think of each person who needs help and make a list. Pray for the people on your list. Then write down some of the key lessons you think each would find most helpful, and find a time when the two of you can talk it all over. Or find another Dave and Teri.

Use your social media contacts and other networks to pass on key ideas that impact you and your understanding of retirement, being faithful for a lifetime.

6) Connect

Please connect with us at RetirementReformation.org to view some of our essays, resources and teaching tools that can help you spread the good news is the retirement Reformation. Download Prayer Mate, and use the devotions and prayer walking outline available on the website.

7) Repeat.

Continue practicing these steps and see how you can bear much fruit by helping more people see and embrace the vast potential that a reformed retirement can offer. The fruit of the spirit will be reflected in your life and the changed lives of others.

Thank you for joining me on this journey. We have come so far, and there is so much more to come. Let's journey together with Trusted advice along The Way.

"I no longer call you servants because a servant does not know his master's business, instead I have called you friend." John 15:15

Friend, remember the definition of ministry is "changed lives." Mine has changed, I pray yours has too, and together we'll impact thousands more. Each of us has the opportunity to find Freedom and Faith ... While we experience the final (and Best) decades of our lives.

Printed in the United States
By Bookmasters